CONFLICTS ON MULTIPLE-USE TRAILS:

Synthesis of the Literature and State of the Practice

Sponsored by The Federal Highway Administration and The National Recreational Trails Advisory Committee

Notice:

This document is disseminated under the sponsorship of the Department of Transportation in the interest of information exchange. The United States Government assumes no liability for its contents or use thereof.

The United States Government does not endorse products or manufacturers. Trademarks or manufacturers' names may appear herein only because they are considered essential to the object of this document.

The contents of this report reflect the views of the authors, who are responsible for the facts and accuracy of the data presented herein. The contents do not necessarily reflect the official policy of the Department of Transportation.

This report does not constitute a standard, specification, or regulation.

Acknowledgments

The large number of people and organizations involved in the research for and writing of this report is an indication of how strongly trail managers and users feel about improving cooperation and sharing on multiple-use trails. Their concern and commitment have earned them the thanks of the trails community. Several contributors deserve special recognition, however. The members of the National Recreational Trails Advisory Committee recognized the need for this baseline information and made this project a high priority. They shared their vast trail contacts and advice and reviewed drafts. Advisory Committee Chair Stuart Macdonald, in particular, provided invaluable guidance and contacts and got the effort off to a solid start. Several individuals deserve special thanks for their efforts in actually gathering the information and producing the report you are holding. Melanie Orwig, graduate student in the Department of Parks, Recreation and Tourism Management at North Carolina State University, made a large number of the contacts with trail managers, gathered and recorded references, and compiled all of the appendix material. Steve Fiala, Trails Specialist with the East Bay Regional Park District, made key contacts in California and contributed valuable material. Many others, too numerous to mention, provided guidance and reviewed drafts. Finally, graduate students Timothy Hopkin and Laurie Sullivan researched and gathered much of the original reference material.

Table of Contents

EXECUTIVE SUMMARY

INTRODUCTION

I. **SYNTHESIS OF THE MULTIPLE-USE TRAIL LITERATURE AND PRACTICE**

    A.   Challenges Faced by Multiple-Use Trail Managers

        Maintaining User Safety
        Protecting Natural Resources
        Providing High-Quality User Experiences
            Threats to Quality Experiences

        Summary

    B.   Ways to Avoid or Minimize Conflicts on Multiple-Use Trails

        Physical Responses
        Management Responses

            Information and Education
            User Involvement
            Regulations and Enforcement

        Summary

    C.   Conclusion

II. **RESEARCH NEEDS IN AVOIDING AND MINIMIZING CONFLICTS ON MULTIPLE-USE TRAILS**

    A.   Challenges Faced by Multiple-Use Trail Managers

        Maintaining User Safety
        Protecting Natural Resources
        Providing High-Quality User Experiences

    B.   Ways to Avoid or Minimize Conflicts on Multiple-Use Trails

        Physical Responses
        Management Responses

            Information and Education

User Involvement
Regulations and Enforcement

Overall Approach

Other Research Needs

C. Conclusion 38

APPENDICES

Appendix 1 National Recreational Trails Advisory Committee

Appendix 2 Organizations to Contact for Additional Information

Appendix 3 Persons Contributing Information for this Report

Appendix 4 List of Existing Trail-Sharing Guidelines and Other Educational Materials

BIBLIOGRAPHY

EXECUTIVE SUMMARY

The National Recreational Trails Advisory Committee identified trail-user conflicts on multiple-use trails as a major concern that needs resolution. The Advisory Committee recognized that there is a significant amount of literature and expertise on this topic, but no one source that summarizes the available information. The Committee asked the Federal Highway Administration to produce a synthesis of the existing research to foster understanding of trail conflicts, identify promising approaches for promoting trail sharing, and identify gaps in our current knowledge. This synthesis is intended to establish a baseline of the current state of knowledge and practice and to serve as a guide for trail managers and researchers.

The challenges faced by multiple-use trail managers can be broadly summarized as maintaining user safety, protecting natural resources, and providing high-quality user experiences. These challenges are interrelated and cannot be effectively addressed in isolation. To address these challenges, managers can employ a wide array of physical and management options such as trail design, information and education, user involvement, and regulations and enforcement.

Past research has consistently found that most outdoor recreationists are satisfied with their recreation experiences. Likewise, most trail experiences on multiple-use trails are probably enjoyable and satisfying. Conflicts among trail users do exist, however, and these conflicts can have serious consequences.

Conflict in outdoor recreation settings (such as trails) can best be defined as "goal interference attributed to another's behavior" (Jacob and Schreyer 1980, 369). As such, trail conflicts can and do occur among different user groups, among different users within the same user group, and as a result of factors not related to users' trail activities at all. In fact, no actual contact among users need occur for conflict to be felt. Conflict has been found to be related to activity style (mode of travel, level of technology, environmental dominance, etc.),focus of trip, expectations, attitudes toward and perceptions of the environment, level of tolerance for others, and different norms held by different users. Conflict is often asymmetrical (i.e., one group resents another, but the reverse is not true).

The existing literature and practice were synthesized into the following 12 principles for minimizing conflicts on multiple-use trails. Adherence to these principles should help improve sharing and cooperation on multiple-use trails.

1. Recognize Conflict as Goal Interference -- Do not treat conflict as an inherent incompatibility among different trail activities, but goal interference attributed to another's behavior.
2. Provide Adequate Trail Opportunities -- Offer adequate trail mileage and provide opportunities for a variety of trail experiences. This will help reduce congestion and allow users to choose the conditions that are best suited to the experiences they desire.

3. Minimize Number of Contacts in Problem Areas -- Each contact among trail users (as well as contact with evidence of others) has the potential to result in conflict. So, as a general rule, reduce the number of user contacts whenever possible. This is especially true in congested areas and at trailheads. Disperse use and provide separate trails where necessary after careful consideration of the additional environmental impact and lost opportunities for positive interactions this may cause.

4. Involve Users as Early as Possible -- Identify the present and likely future users of each trail and involve them in the process of avoiding and resolving conflicts as early as possible, preferably before conflicts occur. For proposed trails, possible conflicts and their solutions should be addressed during the planning and design stage with the involvement of prospective users. New and emerging uses should be anticipated and addressed as early as possible with the involvement of participants. Likewise, existing and developing conflicts on present trails need to be faced quickly and addressed with the participation of those affected.

5. Understand User Needs -- Determine the motivations, desired experiences, norms, setting preferences, and other needs of the present and likely future users of each trail. This "customer" information is critical for anticipating and managing conflicts.

6. Identify the Actual Sources of Conflict -- Help users to identify the specific tangible causes of any conflicts they are experiencing. In other words, get beyond emotions and stereotypes as quickly as possible, and get to the roots of any problems that exist.

7. Work with Affected Users -- Work with all parties involved to reach mutually agreeable solutions to these specific issues. Users who are not involved as part of the solution are more likely to be part of the problem now and in the future.

8. Promote Trail Etiquette -- Minimize the possibility that any particular trail contact will result in conflict by actively and aggressively promoting responsible trail behavior. Use existing educational materials or modify them to better meet local needs. Target these educational efforts, get the information into users' hands as early as possible, and present it in interesting and understandable ways (Roggenbuck and Ham 1986).

9. Encourage Positive Interaction Among Different Users -- Trail users are usually not as different from one another as they believe. Providing positive interactions both on and off the trail will help break down barriers and stereotypes, and build understanding, good will, and cooperation. This can be accomplished through a variety of strategies such as sponsoring "user swaps," joint trail-building or maintenance projects, filming trail-sharing videos, and forming Trail Advisory Councils.

10. Favor "Light-Handed Management" -- Use the most "light-handed approaches" that will achieve area objectives. This is essential in order to provide the freedom of choice and natural environments that are so important to trail-based recreation. Intrusive design and coercive management are not compatible with high-quality trail experiences.

11. Plan and Act Locally -- Whenever possible, address issues regarding multiple-use trails at the local level. This allows greater sensitivity to local needs and provides better flexibility for addressing difficult issues on a case-by-case basis. Local action also facilitates involvement of the people who will be most affected by the decisions and most able to assist in their successful implementation.

12. Monitor Progress -- Monitor the ongoing effectiveness of the decisions made and programs implemented. Conscious, deliberate monitoring is the only way to determine if conflicts are indeed being reduced and what changes in programs might be needed. This is only possible within the context of clearly understood and agreed upon objectives for each trail area.

The available research on recreational conflict is helpful for understanding and managing conflicts on trails. There is a great deal we do not know, however. This report concludes by identifying many conflict-related research topics that have not been adequately explored. Some of this suggested research is theoretical in nature, and some is suggested for applied experimentation by managers in the field.

Trail managers recognize trail conflicts as a potentially serious threat. Many are optimistic, however, and feel that when trail conflict situations are tackled head on and openly they can become an opportunity to build and strengthen trail constituencies and enhance outdoor recreation opportunities for all users.

INTRODUCTION

Conflicts on multiple-use trails have been described "as problems of success -- an indication of the trail's popularity" (Ryan 1993, 158). In fact, the vast majority of trail users are satisfied, have few complaints, and return often. However, conflicts among trail users do occur and can have serious consequences if not addressed. The National Recreational Trails Advisory Committee identified trail-user conflicts on multiple-use trails as a major concern that needs resolution. The Advisory Committee recognized that there is a significant amount of literature on this topic, but no one source summarized the available information. The Committee asked the Federal Highway Administration to produce a synthesis of the existing research to help identify ways to avoid and minimize multiple-use trail conflicts. This synthesis is intended to establish a baseline of the current state of knowledge and practice and to serve as a guide for trail managers and researchers.

Multiple-use trails (often called "shared use," "mutual use," or
"diversified" trails) are becoming the norm. It is increasingly common for trail users to encounter other users (or evidence of use) on trails. Some encounters are with users participating in the same activity, and some are with fellow trail users engaged in different activities. While most trail encounters seem to be pleasant or neutral, some are unpleasant. The conflicts that can result from unpleasant encounters may spoil individual experiences and threaten to polarize trail users who could be working together rather than

at odds with one another. As the number of trail users grows and diversity of trail activities increases, the potential for conflict grows as well. It is the responsibility of managers, researchers, and trail users to understand the processes involved in recreational conflicts and do everything possible to avoid and minimize them on multiple-use trails. This synthesis of literature is one step in that direction. It has two primary goals:

* To guide planners and managers by providing a concise, readable synopsis of the literature and current state of management knowledge regarding how to best accommodate multiple activities on the same trails.

* To direct future research by clearly identifying the topics which most warrant further study, in terms of both formal scientific inquiry and manager experimentation.

Although this report is about conflicts on trails, its tone is intended to be positive, constructive, and hopeful. The nature of a literature review is historic -- what has been tried, what has been learned, and what the experts have concluded. Because it is largely a synthesis of existing information, this report uses the existing language. This language has tended to revolve around the word "conflict," which could set a negative tone if the report were concerned only with existing information. However, the Advisory Committee is looking beyond the past focus on conflict to a new and more positive focus on trail sharing in which conflicts have been minimized or avoided. With such a focus, contacts with other users can more often become a positive part of the trail experience. This positive approach is consistent with the discussions we had with trail managers and advocates across the country. They regard the resolution of trail conflicts as an opportunity to build a stronger, more mutually supportive community of trail users. By focusing on the many things trail users have in common and the many constructive trail-sharing efforts underway across the country, they feel it will be easier to address the relatively few areas that tend to pull users apart.

The scope of this document is broad because conflicts come in many shapes and forms. In fact, the majority of the literature related to conflict and conflict resolution is from the perspective of international politics and organizational behavior. The focus of this report is conflicts on trails. Even in the area of trails, many types of conflicts can occur -- conflicts between trail users and animals, trail users and trail managers, even trail proponents and private landowners, to name just a few. This synthesis recognizes these as important topics, but will only address conflicts among trail users. Although it focuses on conflicts among the users of multiple-use trails, it does so within the context of the other interrelated problems trail managers face. It also uses a broad definition of multiple-use trails and attempts to make applications to a wide variety of different types of trails.

Resolving conflicts and promoting trail sharing among users is only one of many challenges faced by managers of multiple-use trails. In attempting to address the issue of trail conflicts, however, it quickly becomes apparent that the challenges trail managers face are interrelated, as are the tools available to address these challenges. It is superficial to attempt to focus only on how to reduce conflict without also addressing other threats to user satisfaction, issues related to visitor safety, and the impacts trail use has on natural resources. The focus of this report is how to improve trail sharing by avoiding and resolving conflicts. To address this topic adequately, it is presented within the context of these interrelated issues. Similarly, the responses available to address all of these challenges are interrelated and are also presented here.

Likewise, "multiple-use trail" is defined broadly for the purposes of this document. A multiple-use trail is typically defined as any trail that is used by more than one user group, or for more than one trail activity. These two terms are the ones most commonly used to refer to users traveling by different modes of transportation and are used interchangeably in this report. Trail-user groups include hikers, equestrians, mountain bicyclists, cross-country skiers, 4-wheel drive users, off-highway motorcyclists, all-terrain vehicle users, and snowmobilers. Many other trail-user groups exist as well, including in-line skaters, dog sledders, llama packers, and wheelchair users to mention a few. Any trail used by more than one of these user groups is certainly a multiple-use trail. However, when considering trail conflict, we have to consider other trails as well. Even single-use trails must accommodate very different styles of a single activity. A pedestrians-only trail, for example, might be used by hikers, backpackers, trail runners, bird watchers, hunters, snowshoers, orienteers, rock hounds, etc., and conflict can and does occur among any and all of these trail users. Conflicts occur even among members of the same user group. Therefore, the information contained here can and should be applied to all trails since in the broadest sense all trails are multiple-use trails and are being shared to some extent.

A wide variety of trail types were also considered in attempting to address the topic of trail conflicts thoroughly. Information was considered that pertains to trails ranging from hard-surfaced urban greenways to unimproved backcountry trails extending miles from the nearest access point. Although there are obvious physical differences among these many types of trails, much of the information and all of the conclusions reached can be applied successfully to any recreational trail. By definition, a literature review considers the information available. In some parts of the report this fact will tend to emphasize the perspective of one user group or a particular type of trail over others. Much of the most recent information regarding information and education efforts on trails, for example, was written with mountain biking in mind. These apparent biases are simply due to the references available. In most cases, the reader will be able to make broader applications of examples or studies originally directed at a single type of trail or trail-user group.

This report is organized into two parts. Part I presents the synthesis of literature and practice related to multiple-use trails. It is organized around the three major challenges faced by trail managers and the two categories of responses at their disposal to address these challenges. In every case the challenges and available responses cut across many trail activities and types of trails. Part I concludes with a presentation of general principles for avoiding and minimizing conflicts on multiple-use trails distilled from the information reviewed. Part II builds on the synthesis by identifying gaps in our current knowledge and suggesting research that could be undertaken to close these gaps.
This report is a review and synthesis of literature, but the literature considered was more than that typically reviewed for academic purposes. Three types of written and computer-based information sources were reviewed: research-based literature (scientific journals, conference proceedings, technical reports, etc.), management documents, and

popular literature. In addition (and often more helpful), many hours of discussions with trail experts were undertaken, and examples from the field examined. Conducting the research and preparing this report have been a challenging and rewarding endeavor. It is our hope that the information that follows will help you, the trail manager, researcher, or trail user, to understand the dynamics of conflicts on multiple-use trails and the tools available to address this challenge. When addressed head on and openly, the seemingly negative challenge of trail conflicts can become a positive opportunity to improve trail sharing and enhance outdoor recreation opportunities for all users.

> This optimistic sentiment was echoed by several presenters at the Eleventh National Trails Symposium, which had the theme "Trails for All Americans." Their comments are a fitting way to end this introduction and set the tone for the material that follows.
>
> "Communication and cooperation between and among user groups enhances the opportunity for enjoyable trail experiences for all users" (Henley 1992, 171).
>
> "All of us share these common goals: to protect access to public lands, protect the environment and its beauty, to enjoy traveling and being outdoors, to encourage responsible recreation and tourism" (Macdonald 1992, 19).
>
> "Since funding for trails is scarce, we need to find ways of sharing what we do have in a manner which does not infringe upon any one group or groups of users" (Dingman 1992, 168).
>
> "Ignoring, or fighting, entire categories of trail users means losing a great deal of potential support. And it threatens funding and political power by turning the trails community into competitors -- and enables us all to be dismissed as special interest groups" (Macdonald 1992, 19).
>
> "Splintering the outdoor user groups is playing into the hands of those interests that would exploit or destroy the resource we're all preoccupied with saving. The Davids of the world have a tough job already. If we continue to sling rocks at each other, the Goliaths will walk or ride all over us. Let's build trails, not walls, between each other" (John Viehman as quoted in Henley 1992, 174).
>
> "Sharing trails means sharing responsibility for, as well as the use of, our trail system. We can consider responsibility in three phases: my responsibility, your responsibility and our responsibility" (Filkins 1992, 175).
>
> "Reduction in user conflict comes with the recognition of other legitimate trail activities. In a time of increasing population and decreasing trail budgets we must work towards expansion of recreational trails for all rather than restriction of opportunity for some" (Filkins 1994).

I. SYNTHESIS OF THE MULTIPLE-USE TRAIL LITERATURE AND PRACTICE

A. Challenges Faced by Multiple-Use Trail Managers

The manager of any trail faces many challenges, usually within the context of too few staff and too little money. The underlying challenges faced by trail managers, however, remain the same regardless of the type of trail and whether it serves a single group or many different ones. Trail managers attempt to: 1) maintain user safety, 2) protect natural resources, and 3) provide high-quality user experiences. These issues can become more complex and more difficult to manage as the number and diversity of trail uses increase, but the challenges and the tools available to address them remain basically the same.

Maintaining User Safety

Unsafe situations or conditions caused by other trail users can keep visitors from achieving their desired trail experiences. This goal interference due to safety concerns is a common source of conflicts on trails. There are a number of threats to user safety that can occur on trails. Some of these include:

* Collisions and near misses among users and/or their vehicles.
* Reckless and irresponsible behavior.
* Poor user preparation or judgment.
* Unsafe conditions related to trail use (e.g., deep ruts, tracks on snow trail, etc.).
* Unsafe conditions not related to trail use (e.g., obstacles, terrain, weather, river crossings, etc.).
* Poor trail design, construction, maintenance or management.
* Other hazards (e.g., bears, lightning, cliffs, crime, etc.).

To help maintain user safety on trails, planners and managers can attempt to control or influence many factors, including the following:

* User speed (often has more to do with speed *differential* than the speed itself).
* Mass of user and vehicle (if any).
* Sight distances.
* Trail width.
* Trail surface.
* Congestion (e.g., number of users per mile).
* Users overtaking one other silently/without warning.
* Trail difficulty (obstacles, terrain, condition, etc.).
* User skill level and experience.
* User expectations and preparedness (e.g., walkers who understand they may see bicycles on a particular trail can better prepare themselves for possible encounters).
* Emergency procedures.
* On-site management presence.

Protecting Natural Resources

Resource impacts such as soil erosion, damaged vegetation, polluted water supplies, litter, vandalism, and many other indications of the presence of others can lead to feelings of crowding and conflict. These feelings can occur even when there is no actual contact among different trail users. A hiker's enjoyment might be reduced by seeing All-Terrain Vehicle (ATV) tracks near a wilderness boundary, for example, or an equestrian user might be upset to see many cars with bike racks at the trailhead before beginning a ride.

Minimizing environmental impacts is a high priority for resource and recreation managers. Natural resources include soils, wildlife, vegetation, water, and air quality. Historic, cultural, and archaeological resources are also vulnerable to impacts caused by trail use. A considerable amount of trail manager time and resources is spent attempting to minimize impacts affecting each of these resources. All trail use, regardless of travel mode, impacts natural resources. Research indicates that the following factors influence the amount of resource damage caused by trail use:

* Soil characteristics: type, texture, organic content, consistence, depth, moisture (e.g., muddy versus dry), temperature levels (especially frozen versus thawed), etc.
* Slope of surface and topography
* Position in land form (e.g., northern versus southern exposure)
* Elevation
* Type of ecosystem
* Type of wildlife
* Type of vegetation in trail
* Type of vegetation and terrain beside trail (influencing widening)
* Quality of trail design and construction (especially regarding drainage)
* Level of maintenance (e.g., effectiveness of drainage)
* Type of use
* Type of vehicle
* Level of use
* Concentration or dispersal of use
* Season of use
* Difficulty of terrain (to user)
* Up or down hill traffic direction
* Style of use or technique (e.g., skidding tires versus controlled riding)

There is a large body of research regarding the natural resource impacts of outdoor recreation. Much of this research is reviewed in *Visitor Impact Management: A Review of Research*, by Kuss, Graefe, and Vaske (1990). It provides an excellent summary and synthesis of the findings of more than 230 articles related to the vegetation and soil impacts of recreation, 190 related to water resources impacts, and another 100 related to impacts on wildlife. Many of these deal directly or indirectly with trail use. Another excellent reference is a bibliography prepared by the National Off-Highway Vehicle Conservation Council (date unknown). It identifies more than 750 studies relating to off-highway vehicles and their use. A large number of these relate to resource impacts and resource protection.

Based on their thorough review of the literature, Kuss et al. (1990) conclude that evaluations of impacts should be made on a site-specific or area-specific basis due to the many interrelated factors affecting them. They do, however, offer the following generalizations regarding the impacts of various trail uses: backpacking causes more damage than hiking without a pack; hiking and backpacking cause greater changes to trails than walking; horses and packstock cause greater damage than hiking; trail biking causes more damage than hiking; and track-driven vehicles cause more damage than wheel-driven vehicles. They note, however, that site-specific factors can lead to exceptions to these generalizations. In a recent study of erosion damage caused by trail use, Seney (1991) concluded that horses produced more erosion than hikers, off-road bicycles, or motorcycles and that wet trails were more susceptible to damage than dry trails.

It is sometimes difficult to distinguish trail damage caused by trail users from damage caused by nonusers. For example, equestrian trail use is often blamed for damage caused by livestock grazing on public lands. Damage that appears to have been caused by motorized trail users may have been caused by trail crews accessing work sites or by miners traveling to and from their claims. In many cases, the initial construction of the trail itself causes greater resource impact than subsequent trail use (Keller 1990).

One aspect of protecting natural resources that is particularly relevant to multiple-use trail management is the relationship between amount of use and levels of natural resource impact. Numerous studies of the effects of camping indicate that the greatest environmental impact occurs with low use (see review by Kuss et al. 1990). In other words, the initial users of lightly used areas cause the most damage to soils and vegetation. The rate of degradation generally decreases after a certain amount of damage has been done. This has important implications for the issue of whether to concentrate or disperse trail use. In trail settings where this same relationship holds, dispersing trail use to relatively unused trails may greatly increase environmental impacts.

Providing High-Quality User Experiences

Researchers believe that people who participate in outdoor recreation activities do so because they hope to gain certain rewards or outcomes (Vroom 1964; Driver and Tocher 1970). These outcomes consist of a wide variety of experiences such as solitude, challenge, being with friends or family, testing skills, experiencing nature, and others (Driver and Knopf 1977; Driver and Brown 1978; Tinsley and Kass 1978). What experiences are desired vary a great deal across activities, among people participating in the same activity, and even within the same individual on different outings (Schreyer and Roggenbuck 1978; Graefe, Ditton, Roggenbuck, and Schreyer 1981). In fact, recreationists are often seeking to satisfy multiple desires in a single outing (Hendee 1974, Driver and Tocher 1970). So recreation behavior is understood to be goal-directed and undertaken to satisfy desires for particular experiences. The quality of these experiences is often measured in terms of users' overall satisfaction (Williams 1988).

In a perfect world, land managers could provide nearby, high-quality opportunities for every type of experience trail users might possibly seek. This is rarely possible, of course.

Limited budgets, limited amounts of land, and the sheer number of users with different preferences make it impossible to perfectly satisfy all the people all the time. Flexibility, compromise, and common courtesy on the parts of all users are necessary to maximize the opportunities for high-quality experiences for everyone.

Threats to Quality Experiences -- Past research has consistently found that outdoor recreationists are well satisfied with their recreation experiences (Kuss et al. 1990, 191). However, recreation experiences are affected by many subjective as well as situational factors: the conditions encountered at an area, users' expectations, any discrepancies between what users expect and what they actually find or experience (Lawler 1973; Peterson 1974; Schreyer and Roggenbuck 1978; Todd and Graefe 1989), social and personal norms (shared "rules" or "standards" of good or bad, right or wrong, etc.), use levels (Kuss et al. 1990), and "social interference" (Brehm 1966; Proshansky, Ittelson and Rivlin 1970). For a complete review of research related to the recreation experience, see Kuss, Graefe, and Vaske (1990). Two of the most serious threats to quality trail experiences on multiple-use trails are discussed in more detail below.

Crowding -- Crowding is more than the objective density of users in a particular area. It is a subjective judgment on the part of an individual that there are too many other people there. In other words, it is a negative evaluation of a particular density of people in an area (Stokols 1972; Rapoport 1975; Kuss et al. 1990). As such, crowding can reduce the quality of recreation experiences. Level of use does appear to affect feelings of crowding, but in most cases not directly. Levels of perceived crowding vary with such mediating factors as:

* Number of encounters
* Number of encounters preferred
* Number of encounters expected
* Discrepancy between actual and expected encounters
* Motivations for participation (e.g., solitude versus social interaction)
* Preferences (desires)
* Expectations (what was anticipated)
* Behavior (as opposed to the number) of others
* Visitor attitudes
* Type of area (e.g., primitive versus urban)
* Location of contacts (e.g., trailhead versus campsite)
* Proximity of others
* Size of group
* Size of group encountered
* User's experience level
* Perceived environmental disturbance
* Type of encounter
* Obtrusiveness of visual impact (e.g., bright-colored versus earth-toned clothes, tents, and equipment)

See Kuss et al. (1990) for an excellent review and synthesis of research related to crowding. Crowding on trails can be the result of others participating in the same trail activity or different activities. Crowding can be related to feelings of conflict on trails.

Conflict -- The verb "share" is generally defined as "to distribute parts of something among others; to retain one part of something and give the rest or part of the rest to another or others; to take or use a part of something with someone or something; to do or experience something with others; to join with others in doing or experiencing something." On the other hand, the verb " conflict" is defined as "to be at variance, clash, to struggle, or contend" (New Webster's Dictionary 1992). Conflict can cause serious impacts to recreation experiences, to the point of causing some users to end their use and be displaced by other pre-emptive users (Schreyer 1979).

According to recreation researchers, conflict is a special type of dissatisfaction. It is generally defined as "goal interference attributed to another's behavior" (Jacob and Schreyer 1980, 369; Jacob 1977). For example, when a trail user fails to achieve the experiences desired from the trip *and* determines that it is due to someone else's behavior, conflict results and satisfaction suffers. As defined by Jacob and Schreyer (1980), conflict is not the same thing as *competition* for scarce resources. If people attribute not getting a parking place at a trailhead to their *own* lack of planning, there is no conflict. If they *blame* the lack of parking places on horseback riders who they feel have parked their trucks and trailers inconsiderately (whether or not this is truly the case), conflict will likely result. In both cases, users did not achieve their goals, and dissatisfaction resulted, but only one was due to conflict as defined here.

As with crowding, conflict is not an objective state but depends on individual interpretations of past, present, and future contacts with others. Jacob and Schreyer (1980, 370) theorize that there are four classes of factors that produce conflict in outdoor recreation:

* **Activity Style** -- The various personal meanings attached to an activity. Intensity of participation, status, range of experience, and definitions of quality (e.g., experts and novices may not mix well).

* **Resource Specificity** -- The significance attached to using a specific recreation resource for a given recreation experience (e.g., someone running her favorite trail near where she grew up along Lake Tahoe will not appreciate seeing a tourist demonstrate a lack of respect for her "special place" by littering).

* **Mode of Experience** -- The varying expectations of how the natural environment will be perceived (e.g., bird watchers who are "focused" on the natural environment will not mix well with a group of ATV riders seeking speed and thrills who are "unfocused" on the environment).

* **Tolerance for Lifestyle Diversity** -- The tendency to accept or reject lifestyles different from one's own (e.g., some trail users "just don't like" people who do not share their values, priorities, trail activities, etc.).

These four factors have been redefined by Watson, Niccolucci, and Williams (in press) as "specialization level," "definition of place," "focus of trip/expectations," and "lifestyle tolerance." Their research suggests that these factors may be better at predicting *predispositions* toward conflict than predicting actual goal interference.

Notice that none of the above factors thought to produce (or predispose some to) conflict are necessarily related to the particular activity a trail user might be engaged in at the time. Also note that no actual contact need occur for conflict to be felt.

Taking an approach similar to that of Jacob and Schreyer (1980), Owens (1985) attempts to differentiate more clearly between "conflict" and "crowding" from a goal-oriented social and psychological perspective. He defines "recreational conflict" as "a negative experience occurring when competition for shared resources prevents expected benefits of participation from accruing to an individual or group." He defines "social and psychological conflict" as "competition for shared resources amongst individuals or groups whose leisure behavior is mutually exclusive or has contrary objectives and as existing whenever two or more individuals or groups perceive the (recreational) utility of particular (countryside) resources in terms of opposing values or goals." In other words, social interrelationships and differences among users are more the root problem than the physical influences they might have on one another. Owens develops this concept by introducing two propositions:

1. "Conflict is a process of social interaction which is operationalized with the general motivational goal of eliminating environmental instability and restoring perceived equilibrium" (p. 251). According to Owens, all behavior settings have normative "rules." When competing groups view a setting and its purpose in different ways and/or there is inappropriate behavior, these rules begin to break down. In such cases people will employ various coping mechanisms (behavioral, cognitive, or affective) to try to eliminate the source of stress and try to return things to a more desirable state. Conflict occurs when these coping strategies are inadequate, unsuccessful, or unavailable in an acceptable period of time and alternatives seem to be unavailable (i.e., if a person's coping strategies don't work, his feelings of crowding can become feelings of conflict).

2. "Conflict is a cumulative process of social interaction which once established becomes an enduring psychological state guiding the behavior of individuals and/or groups" (p. 252). Owens proposed that this is how conflict can be distinguished from crowding. Crowding is an immediate reaction to present conditions and thus transient. Conflict is more persistent and enduring, lasting beyond a particular outing. Owens sees conflict itself as an experience which can be viewed as a continuum from "simmering discontent and frustration" to confrontation. It may or may not alter actual behavior. If overt confrontation appears, much of the damage of conflict may have already occurred.

Kuss et al. (1990) noted three types of coping strategies, all of which change the character of the experience for the user forced to cope:

* Users re-evaluate the normative definition of what is acceptable (i.e., they adapt

and accept the conditions they find).
    * Users change their behavior (e.g., use less frequently, use at off-peak times, etc.).
    * Users are displaced altogether (i.e., conditions are unacceptable to them, so they stop the activity or stop visiting that area).

In studies of recreationists on trails, rivers, and lakes, several themes and patterns have been found to relate to conflict. These themes tend to support the four theoretical propositions proposed by Jacob and Schreyer (1980) that were discussed above. These themes are:

    * *Level of Technology* -- Participants in activities that use different levels of technology often experience conflict with one another. Examples include cross-country skiers and snowmobilers, hikers and motorcyclists, canoe paddlers and motor boaters, and nonmotorized raft users and motorized raft users (Lucas 1964; Knopp and Tyger 1973; Devall and Harry 1981; Adelman, Heberlein, and Bonnicksen 1982; Noe, Hull, and Wellman 1982; Noe, Wellman, and Buhyoff 1982; Bury, Holland, and McEwen 1983; Gramann and Burge 1981).

    * *Conflict as Asymmetrical*-- Many times, feelings of conflict are one-way. For example, cross-country skiers dislike encountering snowmobilers, but snowmobilers are not as unhappy about encountering cross-country skiers. This type of one-way conflict has been found between many different activities (Stankey 1973; Schreyer and Nielsen 1978; Devall and Harry 1981; Jackson and Wong 1982; Adelman, Heberlein and Bonnicksen 1982). In general, trail users enjoy meeting their own kind, but dislike uses that are faster and more mechanized than their own (McCay and Moeller 1976; Goldbloom 1992).

    * *Attitudes Toward and Perceptions of the Environment* -- Users in conflict have been found to have different attitudes toward the environment (Knopp and Tyger 1973; Saremba and Gill 1991) and may perceive the environment differently. Perceptions may be influenced by when the user first visited the area, with long-time and frequent visitors being most sensitive to contacts with others (Nielsen, Shelby and Haas 1977; Schreyer, Lime and Williams 1984). People who view the environment as an integral part of the experience are more susceptible to conflict than those who see the environment as just a setting for their activity. (Low Impact Mountain Bicyclists of Missoula (LIMB), for example, encourages riders "to use mountain bikes to enjoy the environment, rather than use the environment to enjoy mountain bikes" (Sprung 1990, 29). Some experiences are dependent upon very specific environments. Likewise, people can become attached to particular settings (Williams and Roggenbuck 1989; Moore and Graefe 1994). Some mountain bikers feel hikers are *too* possessive toward trails (Hollenhorst, Schuett and Olson 1993).

    * *Others as Different* -- Users experiencing conflict perceive others to be different from themselves in terms of background, lifestyle, feelings about wilderness, activities, etc. (Adelman, Heberlein and Bonnicksen 1982). However, trail-user groups are sometimes more similar than they believe (Watson, Williams and Daigle 1991). Method of travel and

group size are the most visible cues users can evaluate to determine their similarity to other groups (Kuss et al. 1990). One negative contact can lead some sensitive users to conclude that "all of *them* are rude."

* *Violation of Norms* -- Individuals and groups with different standards of behavior (social and individual norms that define what behavior is appropriate) often conflict with one another (Jacob and Schreyer 1980; Vaske, Fedler and Graefe 1986). Norms of behavior are established through social interaction and refined through an ongoing process. These norms influence how people behave and how they expect others to behave. For example, many fishermen resent canoeists who shout and yell (Driver and Bassett 1975). They apparently hold a norm that boisterous behavior is inappropriate in those situations. The strength of the norm violated (as well as the importance of the goal interfered with) will influence the magnitude of the conflict. Norms appear to be more useful than goals for predicting conflict (e.g., a hiker and a motorcyclist may share the same goals of experiencing nature and escaping from the city but may cause conflict for one another).

* *Level of Tolerance* -- Level of tolerance for others is related to level of conflict (Jacob and Schreyer 1980; Ivy, Steward and Lue 1992). Levels of tolerance vary widely among individuals depending upon personal norms and situational factors such as group size, where the contact occurs, when the user first visited the area, motivations, and frequency of use (Vaske et al. 1986; Shelby and Heberlein 1986). Levels of tolerance are lowest in "wilderness" areas. Assumed images of activities and stereotyping influence tolerance as well (White and Schreyer 1981; Williams 1993). This is consistent with the belief among members of LIMB that Missoula's "live and let live" attitude contributed to their success in minimizing user conflicts on area trails.

* *Environmental Dominance* -- Users who differ in terms of the importance they give to "conquering" the environment are likely to conflict. This is related to the importance of autonomy, control, challenge, and risk-taking goals (Bury, Holland and McEwen 1983).

Another theme related to trail conflict often expressed by trail managers and trail users is the resentment toward newcomers that is often expressed by traditional trail users. This is similar to the "last settler syndrome" (Nielsen, Shelby and Haas 1977) where visitors want a particular place to remain the way is was when they first arrived. The first or traditional users want to be the last ones allowed access. Mountain bikers commonly complain that hikers want to unfairly exclude them from backcountry areas just because bicycle use is new and untraditional. This "last settler syndrome" is particularly acute in areas where one user group has built and/or maintained trails which are later invaded by other types of uses. Managers and new users must be sensitive to the understandable ownership the traditional users feel toward trails they have built and care for. A similar sense of ownership and tradition makes it more difficult to close trails to a particular use once that use is established. The animosity felt by some long-time mountain bikers toward managers of the Mt. Tamalpias area (Marin County, north of San Francisco) is likely magnified by the fact that in the early days of mountain biking, all trails there were open to mountain biking. Single-track trails were subsequently closed to mountain bike use.

In addition to the general causes of conflict summarized above, it is instructive to look at specific factors that lead to feelings of conflict on trails. Sources of conflict can be either willful or innocent. Some users are irresponsible and unfriendly. They behave in ways they know will annoy others or damage resources. Many, however, are simply not aware of how they should behave on trails. Examples of common sources of conflict among trail users reported by trail managers and users include noise, speed, smell of exhaust, surprise, lack of courtesy, trail damage (e.g., erosion, tracks, skid marks, etc.), snow track damage, different (and sometimes unrealistic) expectations, uncontrolled dogs, horse manure, fouled water sources, littering, animal tracks in snow, wild behavior, and lack of respect for others. Flink and Searns (1993) believe conflict results from an increase in demand for trail resources, increased use of existing limited trails, poor management, underdesigned facilities, lack of user etiquette, and disregard for the varying abilities of trail users (p. 194).

A study of readers of Backpacker magazine found that over two-thirds felt the use of mountain bikes on trails was objectionable (Viehman 1990). Startling other trail users, running others off the trail, being faster and more mechanized, damaging the resources, causing erosion, frightening wildlife, and "just being there" were the biggest concerns (Kulla 1991; Chavez, Winter and Baas 1993). Keller (1990) notes that brightly colored clothes, a high-tech look, and the perception of a technological invasion can all be sources of conflict felt by others toward mountain bikers.

Just as some physical damage to trails is not caused by trail users, some conflicts on trails are not due to other trail users at all. Aircraft noise from sightseeing planes and helicopters, for example, is a major irritant to trail users in Hawaii. Noise and smells from nearby roads or developments can have as much or more impact on trail experiences than conflicts with other users.

So, following this collection of items that can cause conflict on trails, the relevant question is, how big a problem is trail conflict? Certainly, conflict is a major problem on some multi-use trails (Flink and Searns 1993). As mentioned earlier, however, past research has consistently found that outdoor recreationists are well satisfied with their recreation experiences (Kuss et al. 1990, 191). This has been found in a variety of settings, including trails. Because the conflict studies noted above were designed to examine recreational conflict, many of them focused on areas where visible conflicts were occurring. These studies do not give a clear picture of the scope of conflict that might be occurring on trails in general. Conflicts are certainly a serious threat to satisfaction, but serious conflicts may not be the norm.

Several studies of multiple-use rail-trails have included questions related to user conflicts. In a survey of rail-trail managers conducted by the Rails-To-Trails Conservancy in 1991, over half of the 83 managers responding reported no conflicts or "few if any" conflicts on their trails. The most common type of conflicts reported were between hikers and bikers, followed by conflicts between equestrians and bikers. Conflicts involving in-line skaters, cross-country skiers, and dogs were also reported. A study of three rail-trails in Iowa, Florida, and California found that users reported little problem with conflict on average. More than 2,000 users were asked to rate "conflicts with other activities" and "reckless behavior of trail users" on a 7-point scale where "1" represented "not a problem" and "7" represented "a major problem." The mean response was less than 2 on each trail for "conflicts with other activities" and ranged from 1.5 to 2.8 for "reckless behavior of trail users" (Moore, Graefe, Gitelson and Porter 1992, III-26). The same study included an open-ended question that asked "What things did you *like* least about the trail?" The top three responses were recorded for each user. Of a total of 2,128 comments, 316 (14.8 percent) related to the behavior of other users. The most common of these (239) were about bicyclists being inconsiderate, riding two-abreast, passing with no warning, going too fast, and other unspecified concerns about bikers. An additional 72 (3.4 percent) identified crowding as the thing liked least. Similar results were found in a study of trail users on 19 multi-purpose pedestrian and bike trails in Illinois (Gobster 1990, 32). "Use problems" (crowding, conflict, and reckless users) received mean ratings of less than 2 on a 5-point scale where "1" represented "not a problem" and "5" represented a "major problem."

A recent National Park Service study of backcountry recreation management provided information related to conflicts on backcountry trails in 93 national parks (Marion, Roggenbuck and Manning 1993). Nine percent of the parks reported that conflicts between horses and hikers were a problem in many or most backcountry areas. Three percent of the parks reported that conflicts between hikers and mountain bikers were a problem in many or most areas. Day users (apparently due to their large numbers), overnight users, horse users, and mountain bikers were all felt to cause visitor conflicts. Day users, overnight users, OHV/ATV users, horse users, and mountain bikers were also reported to create problems through inconsiderate behavior.

Conflicts among trail users are a serious problem in some areas. On Mt. Tamalpias in Marin County, California, for example, "renegade" mountain bikers have allegedly built illegal trails and engaged in vandalism and sabotage to attempt to gain access to single-track trails closed to them. However, there are also areas where users are successfully (and apparently happily) sharing trails. Unfortunately, the existing research does not offer much insight into how widespread a problem recreational conflict is on trails. Many of the managers we talked to felt conflict was a problem. Several also volunteered that they expected conflicts to increase unless they could do something about the problem soon.

Summary

Managers of multiple-use trails face many interrelated challenges. Most important, they must attempt to keep users safe, minimize negative impacts to natural resources, and provide for high-quality visitor experiences. All of these challenges involve managing various types of impacts caused by recreational use. Conflicts among trail users are one of these impacts. After extensively reviewing the recreation literature, Kuss et al. (1990) developed five principles related to the impacts caused by outdoor recreation (pp. 5, 187-188). Although developed to explain the environmental and social impacts of outdoor recreation in general, they apply equally well to the impacts (including conflict) that challenge managers of multiple-use trails in particular. They consider contacts between users and the damage users cause to the environment as "first-order" social impacts (p. 189). They feel these impacts interact to cause combinations of perceived crowding, dissatisfaction, perceived resource impacts, as well as conflicts between users. Their principles can be summarized as follows:

* Recreational use can cause an interrelated set of impacts to occur (e.g., damage to natural resources caused by one group can lead to feelings of conflict or crowding in another group). There is no single predictable response to recreational use.
* Impacts are related to level of use, but the strength and nature of the relationships vary widely and are influenced by many aspects of use intensity and a variety of situational variables.
* Tolerance to impacts vary (e.g., all individuals do not respond the same way to encounters with other visitors, just as all soils or plants react differently to trampling).
* Impacts are activity-specific. Some activities create impacts more quickly or to a greater degree than others. Impacts even from the same activity can vary according to such factors as mode of transportation, characteristics of visitors, party size, and behavior.
* Impacts are site-specific. Given a basic tolerance level to a particular type of recreation, the outcome of use may still depend on the time and place of the encounter or disturbance.

Conflicts on trails can be a serious, complex challenge, but one that must be addressed if users are to have safe, satisfying experiences. The next section details the tools available to address the challenge of conflict on multiple-use trails.

B. Ways to Avoid or Minimize Conflicts on Multiple-Use Trails

As noted earlier, most participants are satisfied with their outdoor recreation experiences. The challenges discussed in the preceding section, however, can lead to severe consequences if not managed properly. In addition, the nature of the recreation experience limits the manager's options in addressing the potential negative impacts of trail use. Freedom, and freedom of choice in particular, are essential for high-quality outdoor recreation on and off trails. Multiple-use trail managers must be sensitive to this fact and avoid restriction and manipulation whenever possible. The "minimum tool rule" proposed by Hendee, Stankey, and Lucas (1990) for wilderness management is an appropriate guideline for the management of most multiple-use trails as well. They advocate using the least intrusive measures (whether physical or managerial) that will still achieve area objectives. This sensitivity is critical to maintaining the freedom and naturalness so important to most trail-based recreation.

A wide variety of possible responses to addressing conflict problems exists. For example, rail-trail managers responding to a survey by the Rails-To-Trails Conservancy listed the following as techniques they use to overcome conflict-related problems on their trails (listed from most to least frequently reported):

* signage
* education
* meeting with user groups
* expanding facilities
* police or ranger patrols
* enforcement of regulations
* brochures articles in newsletters or local newspapers
* imposing speed limits
* volunteer trail patrols
* partial closings
* bicycle bell give-aways

In a recent National Park Service study of backcountry recreation management in 93 national parks (Marion et al. 1993), managers listed the following as actions they had taken to reduce visitor crowding and conflict in backcountry areas (the numbers following each indicate the percent of managers reporting that they used that technique):

* Inform visitors about crowded conditions they may encounter in certain areas (56 percent)
* Encourage quiet behavior and activities (45 percent)
* Inform visitors about conflicting uses they may encounter in certain areas (40 percent)
* Encourage use of less popular access points and backcountry areas (38 percent)
* Encourage off-season use (29 percent)
* Designate trails for different types of visitor use (27 percent)
* Encourage visitors to use natural-colored equipment and clothing (18 percent)
* Encourage weekday use (14 percent)
* Segregate different types of visitor use by geographic area (12 percent)
* Discourage use during peak seasons (12 percent)
* Discourage weekend use (4 percent)
* Encourage outfitters and large groups to use lesser used areas (2 percent).

The following section discusses these and other possible responses managers can take when faced with one or more of the safety, resource protection, or user experience challenges noted in the previous section. These responses are grouped into two broad categories: physical responses and management responses. Management responses are further broken down into three types: information and education, user involvement, and regulations and enforcement. There is considerable overlap between the physical and management responses as well as among the three types of management responses. An effective program will include many different tools.

Strategies will differ depending upon whether the trail is an existing one or one planned for new construction. There is no reason to wait for any problem to occur before taking steps to address it. This is especially true of conflict. It is always better to try to avoid conflict before it becomes a challenge rather than try to reduce it after it is entrenched. Responses may also be affected by factors outside the manager's immediate control.

Occasionally sharing trails is not an option for managers or users such as when a private or corporate landowner agrees to allow only certain activities (e.g., snowmobile use). These situations may occur as conditions of a lease, easement, or other agreement.

A more common situation that can limit managers' options is overall agency policy. See Keller (1990) for an excellent discussion of the two general policy approaches that guide decisions on mountain bike access (and access for other trail activities) to public lands. Keller identifies a "trails open unless declared closed" policy and a "trails closed unless declared open" policy. Although policies can be changed, they form the context within which managers and users must address conflict and promote cooperation.

Note that although many of the following approaches are directed toward trail users, most require action on the part of trail managers as well as users. Some strategies will require training for the managers, staff, and volunteers who implement them. Conflict resolution training for individuals facilitating initial meetings of different user groups would be very helpful, for example. As pointed out by Keller (1990) the land manager's approach to the issue can be every bit as important as the proposal itself (p. 24).

Physical Responses

Proper trail design, layout, and maintenance (or redesign and reconstruction when necessary) are essential for user safety and resource protection and are important contributors to user satisfaction as well. Proper design includes more than aesthetics and minimizing resource impacts. It can be used to encourage trail users to behave in more appropriate ways. Influencing proper behavior through the subtleties of design is preferable and often more effective than attempting to do so after the fact through education programs or regulations. For example, it is easier and more effective to prevent shortcutting of switchbacks by designing climbing turns in rugged, well-screened areas than by posting educational signs at poorly designed switchbacks.

Different users often have very different needs and desires in terms of physical trail attributes such as surface, slope, length, safe sight distances, amenities, etc. Various standards and recommendations are available for different user groups (see American Association of State Highway and Transportation Officials 1991; USDA Forest Service 1991; Flink and Searns 1993; Ryan 1993; Seier 1990). These needs and preferences are far from universal even within one user group, however. Walkers, joggers, runners, hikers, people walking dogs, and people pushing strollers are all pedestrians, for example, but they do not have the same needs and desires in terms of physical trail attributes or trail settings. The best physical responses will always be dictated by specific local conditions. Managers and planners should identify the present and likely future trail users and determine the needs and desires of those users. Users of different ages, motivations, activity preferences, etc., will have different physical trail needs and preferences. Ryan (1993), for example, suggests hosting a "community design workshop" for proposed rail-trails to identify these needs and preferences.

Options. Here is a partial list (in no particular order) of physical design, layout, and maintenance alternatives that can help avoid or minimize trail conflicts:

* Provide adequate trail mileage and a variety of trail opportunities in terms of terrain, difficulty, scenery, etc. Trail impacts, including conflicts, may be due more to the number of users on the trail than the types of users present or their behavior. Therefore, one important physical response option is to provide more trails and perhaps different kinds of trails where possible and appropriate. This will help disperse use and contribute to user satisfaction.

* Use the least intrusive physical manipulation that will achieve area objectives (Hendee, Stankey and Lucas 1990). Some physical solutions can reduce the opportunities for some experiences sought by trail users (e.g., manipulated or hardened surfaces can make solitude and enjoyment of natural surroundings less achievable).

* Provide separate trails when necessary and possible. This may be necessary only for problem sections. In other situations, whole trails or separate systems should be provided for different uses.

Flink and Searns (1993) advocate designing trails with specific users in mind to avoid conflict and unsafe trail conditions. They propose the following six alternative layouts for land-based trails (pp. 208 -- 210).

* *Single Tread, Single Use* -- The Appalachian Trail, for example, is designed and managed primarily for hiking.
* *Single Tread, Multiple Use* -- Almost any urban, multiple-use trail is an example of this type of configuration. The W&OD Trail west of Washington, D.C., for example, is open to walking, running, bicycling, in-line skating, and other uses on the same paved tread.
* *Single Tread Time of Use* -- (i.e., different types of use allowed on the single tread at different times of day, days of week, season of the year, etc.). This concept is similar to swimming pool regulations that set aside certain times for lap swimming only. Snowmobile trails in that are open for multiple use during parts of the year but are restricted to snowmobiling during winter months illustrate this as do multiple-use trails that are set aside for periodic special events such as "walk-a-thons." Beachside trails in southern California that are closed to biking when the lifeguard determines they are too crowded are a form of time zoning. At such times a red light is lit indicating that bikers must walk their bikes.
* *Single Tread, Zoning for Multiple Use* -- (i.e., different types of use allowed on different sections of the trail). For example, the Heritage Trail east of Dubuque, Iowa, has one section set aside for cross-country ski use in the winter while the rest is available for snowmobiles. This type of zoning is also accomplished through design on the Platte River Greenway near Denver. Urban sections are paved and open to most nonmotorized uses, while some more rural sections are surfaced in crusher fines and are unusable by in-line skates and narrow-tired bicycles.

*   *Multiple Tread, Multiple Use* -- (i.e., different treads provided for different types of users within the same corridor). The heavily used Ojai Trail northwest of Los Angeles in Ventura County has adopted this approach. A 10-foot-wide paved trail for bicyclists and pedestrians runs parallel to a 10-foot-wide wood chip trail designed for equestrian use. The two are separated by a 42-inch-high wooden fence. The Venice Beach Trail south of Los Angeles separates two-way bicycle traffic from two-way pedestrian and skater traffic using a yellow center line and stamps on the pavement to indicate appropriate uses within each lane.

*   *Multiple Tread, Single Use* -- (i.e., provide different treads for various skill levels or preferences among the same user type). Urban trails that include a hard-surfaced trail for walkers with a nearby dirt path for runners illustrate this configuration as do cross-country ski areas that provide a set track on one side of a wider platform groomed for "skating."

McCoy and Stoner (1992) feel that providing separate trails for different users groups has many drawbacks, however. They point out that it can be expensive, cause resentment, be difficult to enforce, and limit opportunities for communication and cooperation among users. When separate trails are necessary, they suggest encouraging rather than requiring single use and explaining the reasons for this strategy at trailheads. This approach combines physical design with information and education efforts. Advocates of multiple-use trails see providing separate trails as a last resort. They feel positive interactions among users on the trail is the best way to foster communication, understanding, and a strong, cooperative trail community.

*   Paint a centerline on heavily used multi-purpose greenways. This can help communicate that users should expect traffic in both directions (Flink and Searns 1993) and encourage users to travel on the right and pass on the left.
*   Screen trails for sight, sound, and smells (e.g., exhaust fumes from motorized vehicles). Design in buffers (physical, visual, etc.) by using topography, vegetation, the sound of rivers, etc. to insulate users from one another when possible. Add buffers as needed on existing trails.
*   Provide separate trailheads for different users.

*   Separate uses at trailheads and for the first (most crowded) stretches of the trail. These separate segregated trails could then converge, perhaps a mile from the trailhead, after users are more spread out. On the other hand, Attila Bality of the National Park Service Southwestern Region advocates forcing all trail users to share the same trail for some distance (e.g., a mile) before having single-use or restricted-use trails diverge from the main trail if necessary. His feeling is that users will only learn to understand one another and share trails if encouraged to do so. Some may not share unless forced to do so.
*   Design in adequate sight distances.
*   Build trails wide enough to accommodate the expected use. Many sources and recommended standards are available for various user groups (see American Association of State Highway and Transportation Officials 1991; USDA Forest Service 1991; Flink and Searns 1993; Ryan 1993).

* Build trails wide enough for safe passing, and/or provide pullout areas.

* Design and construct trails to minimize erosion. Resource damage attributable to a particular user group can cause conflict as well. Numerous excellent sources of information are available regarding trail construction and maintenance techniques (See Flink and Searns 1993; Ryan 1993; Albrecht 1992; American Hiking Society 1990; USDA Forest Service 1991; USDA Forest Service 1984; Proudman and Rajala 1981; Birchard and Proudman 1981). Some recommended actions to control erosion are:

-- Drain the surface -- design for drainage, and install drainage structures where needed. Excellent suggestions for options on mountain bike trails are included in McCoy and Stoner (1992).

-- Avoid steep grades.

-- Use full bench construction (full trail tread supported by undisturbed soil rather than fill) when possible.

-- Design trails *across* slopes, not parallel to the fall line.

-- Keep trails (especially inclines) in areas of erosion-resistant soils.

-- Use trail-hardening techniques where appropriate (e.g., geo-tech fabrics, turf stone or tread support blocks, etc.).

-- Minimize erosion at switchbacks on mountain bike trails by keeping surface rough (slow speeds prevent mountain bikers from locking brakes), providing rock and log barriers at edges to prevent shortcutting and speeding to outer edge, or using climbing turns instead.

* Design to control speeds where necessary (e.g., where mountain bikes are sharing trails with walkers). Obviously, these techniques should only be used in situations where they will not create a safety hazard. To control speeds, managers have attempted to:

-- Vary the trail surface (e.g., add aggregate).

-- Vary the trail terrain (e.g., no banked turns).

-- Design to include frequent turns. But avoid sharp turns after long straight sections on mountain bike trails since fast riders may lock their brakes and skid into these turns.

-- Add or leave barriers (e.g., rocks, roots, bumps, curves, washboard surfaces, downed trees, narrow sections, waterbars, and other drainage structures, bumps, or "roll and dip" sections as described by McCoy and

Stoner 1992). Be aware, however, that the Americans With Disabilities Act prohibits building barriers that would make a facility less accessible to persons with disabilities.

--   Where trail systems consist of a combination of single-track and road sections, design and manage so that single-track sections are traveled uphill and the roads downhill. This will slow mountain bikes on narrow sections and reduce skidding.

*   Design entrances to and exits from loops at angles to encourage one-way traffic where desired. (This reduces the problem of signing for one-way traffic, which may lead some users to let down their guard and not expect the oncoming traffic which may still occur.)

*   Provide adequate facilities (toilets, places to tie horses, etc.).

*   Have an effective maintenance program appropriate to the type of trail and its use. Flink and Searns (1993, 298-- 299) consider such programs essential for users' safety and experiences and provide an excellent example for greenways. According to Ryan (1993), trail maintenance programs should address, at a minimum, the following: signs and markings, sight distance and clearance, surface repair, drainage, sweeping and clearing, structural deterioration, and illumination. She suggests involving the public in these activities through adopt-a-trail or similar programs.

Management Responses

Once a trail is physically in place, managers can still have a tremendous influence on user safety, natural resource protection, and user experiences. Management actions can take many forms, from doing nothing to closing areas. The alternatives can be grouped into three categories: information and education, user involvement, and regulations and enforcement. Considerable overlap exists among these three groups, of course. This is especially true of information/education and user involvement (e.g., a volunteer trail patrol provides information and educates users, involves users in taking responsibility for their own trails and use, and may well assist in communicating and enforcing regulations and preventing resource damage). Information and education, user involvement, and regulations and enforcement are discussed separately below.

Information and Education -- Uninformed, unintentional, unskilled, and careless actions by users are often cited as the causes of many problems in outdoor recreation areas (Roggenbuck 1992; Roggenbuck and Ham 1986). Many managers feel that this is particularly true of trail-related problems. If this is true, educating the public and persuading them to act responsibly should be effective strategies for improving behavior on trails. According to McCoy and Stoner (1992), "effective communication is the best way to prevent user dissatisfaction and conflict." Ryan (1993) advocates education as the key to solving problems associated with mountain bike use and for promoting trail-user etiquette. Many others echo the importance of trail-user education (Merriman 1988).

Whether the behavior being promoted is called trail etiquette, trail ethics, trail courtesy, or trail sharing, information and education efforts are almost universally supported as an essential strategy for providing opportunities for high-quality recreation experiences. Influencing human behavior through information and education is an attractive alternative to controlling or coercing compliance through more heavy-handed techniques that can impact recreation experiences (Manfredo 1992; Lucas 1981). This preference is strongly held by recreationists (Roggenbuck and Ham 1986) and seems to be shared by most managers. Like other good things, however, even information and education can be overdone. Lucas (1981) cautions managers against providing too much information, especially in backcountry settings where users may be seeking discovery and exploration.

Considerable literature exists on the use of information and education in recreation settings. An excellent reference is *Influencing Human Behavior: Theory and Applications in Recreation, Tourism, and Natural Resources Management*, edited by Manfredo (1992). Particularly relevant is the chapter by Roggenbuck entitled, "Persuasion to Reduce Resource Impacts and Visitor Conflicts." He notes that a user's motive for engaging in undesirable behavior will influence how effective persuasion will be in changing the behavior. In terms of the five types of undesirable visitor actions identified by Hendee et al. (1990), Roggenbuck proposes that persuasive communication has low potential for influencing illegal or unavoidable (e.g., human waste) acts, but has very high potential for changing uninformed acts. Similarly, persuasion has moderate potential to influence careless acts (e.g., littering) and high potential of modifying unskilled actions. Gramann and Vander Stoep (1987) categorize violations of norms in parks into six types. Roggenbuck places them in the following order in terms of how effective persuasive communication would be in altering each. From the least likely to be influenced by persuasion to the most likely, they are: status-conforming (i.e., do it to be "in" with the group), willful, releasor-cue (e.g., seeing others do it), responsibility-denial, unintentional, and uninformed.

Roggenbuck (1992) identifies three distinct conceptual routes to persuasion and learning. Each has relevance to designing effective information and education efforts to promote trail sharing.

* Applied Behavior Analysis -- This approach addresses the user's behavior itself and not beliefs, attitudes, thoughts, or values that may be associated with it. This is most frequently attempted through rewards, punishments, manipulation of the environment, or behavioral prompts (e.g., written or oral messages that state "Share the Trail"). Because this approach does not deal with underlying beliefs or attitudes, however, it is not likely to bring about long-term changes in behavior.

* Central Route to Persuasion (also called the "central route to attitude change" by Petty, McMichael and Brannon 1992) -- This approach attempts to change behavior by changing the attitudes and beliefs related to them. It attempts to get recipients to consider the message more carefully and then agree with it. If recipients consider the message and agree with it, they change their beliefs and then act accordingly (one hopes in more desirable ways). In other words, get users to consciously consider their actions

rather than spontaneously engage in behavior that may be undesirable (Vincent and Fazio 1992). The central route to persuasion should have better long-term effects because users' new beliefs and attitudes guide their behavior now and in the future. For example, if a user considers and agrees with a campaign promoting an attitude of "Treat Other Trail Users the Way You Would Like To Be Treated," they might internalize the message and act more considerately in the future. To be effective, the user must be motivated to pay attention, be able to understand and process the message, and have the necessary skills and abilities to respond. According to Roggenbuck, the effectiveness of the persuasion will be influenced by characteristics of the recipient, the message, and the situation. Low-knowledge, first-time users are generally easiest to persuade. Strong, well-supported, specific, clear, relevant, interesting messages tailored to particular audiences are most effective. Well-timed situations with adequate time and few distractions are needed for central route persuasion.

   *   Peripheral Route to Persuasion (also called the "peripheral route to attitude change" by Petty, McMichael and Brannon 1992) -- This approach applies when users are unable or unwilling to give the message their attention or consideration. Therefore, little attitude change or long-term effect is achieved. When users are overloaded with information, they often block out managers' messages or use simple decision rules (e.g., is the source credible or important?) to determine their response. For users in a crowded and distracting trailhead parking lot, for example, a poster of Clint Eastwood with the caption, "Good guys share trails," may be more effective than a carefully thought out, well-supported trail-sharing brochure. Timing and some (but not too much) repetition of the message are critical to the success using the peripheral route to persuasion.

The following information and education advice offered by Roggenbuck and Ham (1986) applies well to any such efforts to reduce trail conflict or promote trail sharing:

Programs become feasible and effective when managers are able to identify clientele groups and their characteristics, place information where people can easily receive it, provide information early in the decision-making process, and present the information in an interesting and understandable way (p. Management-62).

Identifying the particular users in need of the information is a critical and often overlooked part of the education process. For example, Matheny (1979) found that 14- to 17-year-olds were the users most likely to shortcut switchbacks on trails. A successful campaign to reduce shortcutting of trail switchbacks would specifically target those users and do so in ways that would be interesting and compelling to them. Similarly, information and education efforts to avoid or reduce trail conflicts should be directed at the particular users involved.

Information and education programs related to promoting trail sharing should have one or more of the following objectives:

   *   Communicate *why* the trail is shared (Reese 1992).
   *   Communicate that cooperation can benefit all. Skye Ridley, executive

director of the Pikes Peak Area Trails Coalition, notes that the challenge is to convince people that "it's cool to share trails."

* Teach about other users (especially similarities among users). One study found mountain bike riders to be similar to hikers in many respects. Although the riders had fairly accurate perceptions of these similarities, the hikers did not (Watson, Williams, and Daigle 1991). Determining the similarities among different user groups and documenting the extent to which trail users participate in multiple trail activities could ease "us and them" feelings and reduce conflict.

* Communicate the consequences of problem behaviors (e.g., from impact on other users to loss of access for offenders).

* Build consideration and trust.

* Teach trail ethics, including the following:

    - Courtesy toward other trail users and concern toward the environment (Keller 1990).

    - Who should yield to whom and why.

    - Respect and tolerance for others.

    - Responsibility for resource protection.

    - What interferes with other activities.

* Communicate physical and social trail conditions to help users have more accurate expectations of what and whom they are likely to find on a particular trail:

    - Difficulty (grade, length, tread, etc.).

    - Trail length and location.

    - What types and numbers of users might be encountered. Ivy, Steward, and Lue (1992) suggest communicating worst-case scenarios to boaters to allow users to adjust their goals more appropriately. Some managers point out that users have to be realistic and understand that they will sometimes run into the "few bad apples" that exist in every user group.

* Teach what causes resource impacts and how to minimize them (e.g., "stay on the trail," "don't skid down hills," etc.).

* Reach users as early as possible. Many managers feel conflicts are most severe near trailheads since users tend to be most congested there. They suggest focusing education efforts at trailheads and in the first mile or two of trail.

Trail etiquette and trail-sharing guidelines are found in many brochures and other literature produced by a wide variety of trail organizations and management agencies. Appendix 4 contains a comprehensive list of specific examples of written materials that deal directly or indirectly with avoiding or reducing trail conflicts by promoting responsible trail use, trail sharing, etiquette, use dispersal, low-impact use, etc. The names of the organizations producing them are included, and their addresses can be found in Appendix 2.

In addition to the existing programs and literature just noted, trail managers and advocates use many other strategies for communicating with and educating trail users. Many of these are listed below. Some are noted by Kulla (1991), Ryan (1993), and Martin and Taylor (1981), while the majority were suggested in conversations with trail managers. Using a combination of the following approaches will produce better results than relying on only one or two techniques. Alternatives include:

* Posters.
* Brochures, flyers, pamphlets, newsletters, and other printed materials.
* Maps, guidebooks, visitors' guides, etc. These can incorporate trail regulations, low-impact and shared-use messages, information to disperse use, alternative routes, as well as the reasons for the regulations.
* Interpretive rides/walks/etc., by land management staff.
* Presentations before clubs, retailers, school groups, etc.
* Videos (e.g., "In Their Shoes" produced by Arizona State Committee on Trails).
* Volunteer trail patrols.
* "User swaps." This concept builds on the very successful "ROMP and STOMP" events named after the social gatherings between an equestrian group and a mountain bike club called Responsible Organized Mountain Pedalers (ROMP) in California. These joint rides and social events promoted communication between the groups, gave users the opportunity to try the other's trail activity, and also desensitized the horses to mountain bikes. This concept can be extended to become user swaps between any or all trail activities.

* Slide shows.
* Multi-use trail educational kits for schools (Isbill 1993).
* Joint planning meetings.
* Public meetings.
* Role modeling by rangers and others.
* Personal requests and information from peers.
* Leafletting on or off the trail (most appropriate at trailheads, equipment stores, etc., rather than on the trail itself).
* "Trail Days" events.
* "Safety Days" on the trail for presentations, workshops (e.g., radar checks to teach bicyclists what the speed limit feels like when they are riding), fun, and public relations.
* Information sent to recent purchasers of trail vehicles, bicycles, or equipment.
* Trained personnel (staff or volunteers) stationed at trailheads, visitor centers, campgrounds, etc. (e.g., use backcountry rangers or other trail staff/volunteers to inform and educate users about trail sharing).

* Fact sheets.
* Articles in magazines, newspapers, and other mass media outlets.
* Educational "roadblocks" on trails.
* Classes by retailers, land managers, or trail groups to teach trail techniques and trail ethics, communicate area policies, etc.
* Multi-use surveys at trailheads.
* Similarities among user groups communicated and emphasized. The "Mountain Bike Action Kit," for example, suggests that bicyclists attending meetings or hearings "try not to look like bicyclists at all!" (Bicycle Federation of America 1990, 7).
* Understanding of other user groups' concerns.
* Attendance at other trail-user groups' meetings.
* One-on-one peer education on the trail.
* Bumper stickers or window stickers.
* "Hang tags," developed by LIMB for bikes sold or repaired in its area, have a mountain bike code of etiquette on one side and a "positive people interaction" or "care for the land" message on the other. This approach is also used by Recreational Equipment, Inc. (REI).
* Workshops on low-impact use, trail sharing, etc.
* Theme events to enhance activity image (e.g., "bike for birds").
* New users recruited and educated.
* Public service announcements (PSAs).
* Informational signs.
* Signs with positive messages and images for sport (e.g., promoting responsible mountain biking).
* "Burma Shave" signs (i.e., an entertaining, sequential series of signs).
* "No Trace Race" or "No Trace Ride" events to provide a fun way to communicate low-impact messages (Kulla 1991).
* Positive messages/images promoted by equipment manufacturers in their advertising. This is done effectively by the National Off-Highway Vehicle Conservation Council.
* Accurate information provided to users so they know what encounters to expect on particular trails.
* Water bottles printed with "Rules of the Trail."
* Contests and awards for individuals or groups.

When asked how they promoted trail etiquette, a survey of rail-trail managers conducted by the Rails-To-Trails Conservancy in 1991 found that numerous methods were being used on rail-trails. The 78 managers responding listed the following techniques. They are arranged here from the most to the least frequently reported: signs, brochures, ranger patrols, trail guides, presentations to civic groups, presentations to children, visitor contact areas, volunteer patrols, surveys, striping the trail surface, press releases, and trail-user groups/word of mouth. When asked which of these were the most effective, ranger patrols were mentioned most frequently followed by signs and brochures.

User Involvement -- In many respects, user involvement is a special, intensive kind of active, hands-on user education. By actively involving users in trail planning, management, or conflict resolution, they are forced to work together and, as a result, can begin to better understand and appreciate one another's needs, expectations, and perspectives (e.g., user swaps such as "ROMP and STOMP" events). Trail advocates, planners, and managers should attempt to work with unaffiliated individual users and/or with organized user groups before resorting to obtrusive regulations or trail closures. There are obvious efficiencies in working with organizations, but attempts should also be made to involve unaffiliated users. These independents are often less informed and more in need of education. There may also be cases, however, where members of an organized group have negative attitudes toward other users or are uncooperative (Owens 1985). In these cases as well, working with unaffiliated users is essential.

There are many compelling reasons to involve trail users in trail planning and management. Most important, involving users does the following:

* Gives different users the opportunity to learn about and work with one another.
* Gives different users the opportunity to understand one another's needs and see their similarities with one another.
* Builds understanding, cooperation, and trust through working together.
* Gives trail advocates, planners, and managers an efficient channel to learn from users and communicate with them.

There are numerous options for *how* to involve trail users. The following strategies are effective ways of involving users in any aspect of trail planning or management. They can be used to involve any trail-user group or can be used as ways to get different user groups to interact constructively. Options include:

* Public meetings (although this approach often is not seen as a means for involving users for the long term, it can be used as one way of initiating many of the approaches that follow).
* Trail advisory councils composed of representatives of various user groups.
* Joint trail construction or maintenance projects among different user groups.
* Joint trail construction or maintenance skills workshops among different user groups.
* "Trail Days" events sponsored jointly by different user groups.
* Joint fundraising or lobbying efforts.
* "Adopt-a-trail" efforts.
* Volunteer trail groups. They can be organized around a particular trail (the Bay Area Ridge Trail Council is an excellent example), a single trail activity, a coalition of different activities, etc.
* Cooperative lobbying for trails.
* Cooperation among organizations on trail planning.
* Volunteer trail patrols.
* "ROMP and STOMP" events.
* Volunteer "Host" programs.
* Land manager trail walks with affected user groups to discuss problems and

explore solutions (Keller 1990).

* Issues identification workshops, community design workshops, public hearings, citizen advisory committees, surveys, and mass media outreach are all suggested as effective public involvement tools for creating or managing multi-use trails (Ryan 1993).

With any user involvement effort, it is essential to involve the right users early on. Recruiting users who are open-minded, constructive, and willing to work together will make creative and successful solutions much more likely. The East Bay Regional Park District, for example, credits much of the success of its volunteer trail patrol to the hand-picked group of constructive equestrian and mountain bike leaders they recruited to head up the program.

Involving trail users early on sometimes means that the users themselves must initiate their own involvement efforts. For example, the International Mountain Bicycling Association (IMBA) and the Sierra Club, a vocal opponent of mountain bikes on trails, recently began a series of meetings to try to resolve their differences. The meetings are being facilitated by professional mediators and will attempt to establish an ongoing dialogue, develop mutually agreeable standards and policies, and begin a joint public mountain biking education program. Recreation Equipment, Inc. (REI), is underwriting the meetings (IMBA 1993).

Regulations and Enforcement -- There will always be some who cannot be influenced by positive, less forceful means of persuasion (Baker 1990; Watson, Williams and Daigle 1991). Most trail-sharing programs will not succeed without regulations and effective enforcement for those whose lack of consideration could negate the positive impact made by the majority. Regulations and enforcement efforts are most effective when developed and implemented with the input and cooperation of affected user groups (Ryan 1993 Kepner-Trego Analysis 1987). It is also important to communicate to users the *reasons* for any regulations adopted. This will help minimize misunderstandings and confusion among those affected (McCoy and Stoner 1992). However, it is important to re-emphasize that excessive regulations and enforcement can spoil recreation experiences for many users. Conflict with other users could be effectively reduced through elaborate surveillance systems and heavy-handed enforcement where all inconsiderate users were immediately "cuffed and stuffed" into awaiting police cruisers. But the freedom and sense of escape so many trail users seek would be lost. Only the minimum intrusion necessary to achieve area objectives should be employed.

* *Regulations* -- Well thought out regulations provide managers and their staffs with the authority to enforce safe and courteous trail behavior (Flink and Searns 1993) and help clarify for users what is expected of them. Regulations should be posted prominently at trailheads and other appropriate locations. There are three broad areas of regulations that managers often consider.

* *Speed limits* -- Controlling vehicle speeds on trails is essential for user safety as well as the peace of mind of other users. Although education can be effective in this regard, speed regulations are sometimes necessary. Ryan (1993) cautions that

speed limits should be used only as a last resort since they require consistent, ongoing enforcement, may not improve real or perceived safety on the trail, and may discourage bicyclists from using trails for commuting. Addressing mountain biking in particular, Kulla (1991) suggests that speeds must allow riders to stop in one-half the distance they can see. Keller (1990) considers a single speed limit for an entire trail unreasonable and advocates basing limits on sight distances and other trail features.

* *Zoning* -- Separating users can be an effective way of minimizing contacts and reducing conflicts. This approach is not without its critics, however. Arbitrary zoning may unnecessarily restrict use if the potential for conflict is low (Owens 1985). Segregating, restricting, or prohibiting users is advocated only as a last resort by Keller (1990), who suggests dispersing use to guard against concentrating mountain bikes on a small number of trails and possibly increasing impacts there. Where appropriate, zoning can be organized around:

   -- Time of use (by day/week/month/season/year/etc.).

   -- Trail section (e.g., snowmobiling on half of a trail and cross-county skiing on the other half).

   -- Activity.

   -- Type of trail experience sought. For example, some areas can be set aside where conditions are best for solitude, self-reliance, and challenge while other areas can be managed for more comfortable, secure, and social experiences. The USDA Forest Service and Bureau of Land Management accomplish this by using the Recreation Opportunity Spectrum (ROS) to plan for and zone a continuum of different settings areas where conditions are most conducive for achieving different types of experiences (Clark and Stankey 1979). The six classes of settings are "Primitive," "Semi-Primitive Non- Motorized," "Semi-Primitive Motorized," "Roaded Natural," "Rural," and "Urban." The following factors are considered and managed when assigning areas to particular classes and managing them to provide the desired experiences: access, remoteness, naturalness, facilities and site management, social encounters, visitor impacts, and visitor management. Acknowledging that the products of recreation (and trail) outings are *experiences*, and planning and managing to provide for a wide range of opportunities for different experiences is more realistic than managing for different *activities* (e.g., hiking, off-road motorcycling, hunting, etc.). Trail users participating in the same activities do not all desire the same trail experiences. See Hammitt (1988) for use of the ROS as a means of analyzing and managing conflict potential.

* *Right-of-Way* -- Regulations on who must yield to whom are helpful. For example, the IMBA "Triangle" could be enforced, whereby bicyclists yield to pedestrians, and pedestrians and bicyclists both yield to horseback riders. Some managers would also like to see this modified into a "Yielding Square" that would include the responsibilities of

motorized users to those they meet on the trails.

The following are other examples of regulations that have been or could be established for multiple-use trails:

* Forbid cutting of switchbacks.
* Mandate one-way travel on certain trails.
* Require bicyclists to walk their bikes in congested or conflict-prone areas or during congested times.
* Require bicycles to have bells as is now the case on trails managed by the East Bay Regional Park District in California.
* Close trails or trail sections during sensitive seasons (e.g., muddiest times or wildlife breeding times).
* Charge user fees (to help fund trail programs or disperse use).
* Designate appropriate places to tie horses.
* Require completion of a trail-sharing and/or minimum impact course to be eligible for a mandatory trail permit.
* Require users to repair any impacts their use might have caused (e.g., after a major motorcycle event or large group equestrian event).
* Require users to stay on the trails.
* Close certain sections, areas, or types of trails (e.g., no mountain bikes on crowded single-track trails).
* Enact a "Model Path User Ordinance" like that of King County, Washington, which contains 10 articles covering issues from littering to respect for other users.

Enforcement -- How to gain compliance with necessary regulations has been a great challenge in many trail areas. This is especially true where land areas are large and budgets are lean. The following are important considerations for determining how to enforce regulations on trails:

* Inform users of the regulations:

    -- Post regulations at trailheads and include them in trail brochures and on maps (Ryan 1993). Ryan also suggests communicating why and how the regulations will be enforced and what the applicable penalties are.
    -- Post and enforce regulations from the very beginning on newly opened trails. Establishing desirable patterns of behavior from the start is far easier than trying to change bad user habits later on.
    -- Some feel using wordings such as "Not Recommended" rather than "No" in messages produces a more cooperative atmosphere and better compliance (McCoy and Stoner 1992). Many managers, however, feel that offending users will take advantage of more lenient wordings.

* Communicate the *reasons* for regulations to the users affected. For example, communicating to mountain bikers that "up trail and down road" rules for travel directions are enforced to help keep speeds at safer levels and skidding at a minimum

may help with compliance.

* Enforce rules and regulations consistently to assure that there is no perception of discrimination among different user groups.

* Employ a variety of on-site enforcement personnel if possible and appropriate:

    -- Peer policing programs (e.g., peer pressure).
    -- Volunteer trail patrols.
    -- Uniformed enforcement officers.
    -- Cooperative agreements with local law enforcement and fire protection agencies.

* Consider sentencing trail offenders to work service on the trail as part (or all) of their penalty (Goldstein 1987 as cited in Keller 1990).

* Communicate emergency procedures for users and emergency personnel.

Summary

The previous section presents some of the many physical and management responses available to attempt to avoid and minimize conflicts on multiple-use trails. All of these have been employed on multiple-use trails with varying degrees of success. The right choice for any particular situation will depend on many local factors and involve some experimentation. General principles to guide responses are offered in the next section. In general, though, using a strategy that employs a combination of techniques with a long-term perspective is best. The city of Edmonton, Alberta, for example, has had good results with an integrated program of design, social marketing, education, regulation, and enforcement for its trail system.

Unfortunately, there are cases where conflict has degenerated to the point where the only feasible recourse is direct intervention by experts trained in conflict resolution. Even binding arbitration may be necessary and appropriate in some cases where the techniques mentioned above were employed too late or too tentatively.

C. Conclusion

Multiple-use ("shared-use") trails are an efficient, economical, and increasingly common way to provide trail opportunities. Due to limited rights-of-way, multiple-use trails are sometimes the only alternative. Through thoughtful planning and diligent management, such trails can provide safe, high-quality recreation experiences without unacceptable damage to natural resources. However, the conflicts that sometimes accompany shared use of trails can be very emotional and are not issues that managers are likely to eliminate altogether. With time, patience, commitment, and cooperation among users and between users and managers (McCoy and Stoner 1992) as well as diligent and aggressive planning and management, shared-use trails can be an excellent way to accommodate many types of users with minimal conflict.

There is no one best way to accommodate multiple uses on the same trail while at the same time avoiding (or at least minimizing) conflicts. The best approach will always be dictated by local conditions and the resources available. However, the literature reviewed and the trail manager input received do provide considerable guidance. Based on this information, 12 principles are offered for minimizing conflicts on multiple-use trails.

1. Recognize Conflict as Goal Interference -- Recreational conflict can best be understood as "goal interference attributed to another's behavior" (Jacob and Schreyer 1980, 369). Therefore, trail conflicts are possible among different user groups, among different users within the same user group, and as a result of factors (e.g., lack of tolerance for others) not related to a user's trail activity at all.

2. Provide Adequate Trail Opportunities -- Offer adequate trail mileage and provide opportunities for a variety of trail *experiences*. This will help reduce congestion and allow users to choose the conditions that are best suited to the experiences they desire. As in the Recreation Opportunity Spectrum (ROS), this will require a focus on trail *experiences* as opposed to trail activities. Opportunities for different trail experiences can be maximized by providing trails that vary in terms of terrain, difficulty, access, remoteness, naturalness, facilities and site management, social encounters, visitor impacts, and visitor management.

3. Minimize Number of Contacts in Problem Areas -- Each contact among trail users (as well as contact with evidence of others) has the *potential* to result in conflict. So, as a general rule, reduce the number of user contacts whenever possible. This is especially true in congested areas and at trailheads. Disperse use and provide separate trails where necessary after careful consideration of the additional environmental impact this may cause. Recognize that separating trail users may limit opportunities for communication, understanding, and eventual cooperation among different user groups.

4. Involve Users as Early as Possible -- Identify the present and likely future users of each trail and involve them in the process of avoiding and resolving conflicts as early as possible, preferably before conflicts occur. For proposed trails, possible conflicts and their solutions should be addressed during the planning and design stage with the involvement of prospective users (Ryan 1993, 79). New and emerging uses should be anticipated and addressed as early as possible with the involvement of participants. Likewise, existing and developing conflicts on present trails need to be faced quickly and addressed with the participation of those affected.

5. Understand User Needs -- Determine the motivations, desired experiences, norms, setting preferences, and other needs of the present and likely future users of each trail. This "customer" information is critical for anticipating and managing conflicts. This process must be ongoing and will require time, patience, effort, and sincere, active listening.

6. Identify the Actual Sources of Conflict -- Help users to identify the specific tangible causes of any conflicts they are experiencing (e.g., "teenagers partying and littering at Liberty Campground," "horses fouling the water at Peabody Spring," "mountain bikers speeding down the last hill before the Sills Trailhead," etc.). In other words, get beyond emotions and stereotypes as quickly as possible, and get to the roots of any problems that exist.

7. Work With Affected Users -- Work with all parties involved to reach mutually agreeable solutions to these specific issues. Users who are not involved as part of the solution are more likely to be part of the problem now and in the future. For example, the Bay Area Ridge Trail Council is considering "full and balanced representation" of key user groups on its county committees as it plans sections of its new trail (Isbill 1993).

8. Promote Trail Etiquette -- Minimize the possibility that any particular trail contact will result in conflict by actively and aggressively promoting responsible trail behavior. Use existing educational materials or modify them to better meet local needs. Target these educational efforts, get the information into users' hands as early as possible, and present it in interesting and understandable ways (Roggenbuck and Ham 1986).

9. Encourage Positive Interaction Among Different Users -- Trail users are usually not as different from one another as they believe. Providing positive interactions both on and off the trail will help break down barriers and stereotypes, and build understanding, good will, and cooperation. This can be accomplished through a variety of strategies such as sponsoring "user swaps," joint trail building or maintenance projects, filming trail-sharing videos, and forming Trail Advisory Councils.

10. Favor "Light-Handed Management" -- Use the most "light-handed approaches" that will achieve area objectives (Hendee, Stankey, and Lucas 1990). This is essential in order to provide the freedom of choice and natural environments that are so important to trail-based recreation. Intrusive design and coercive management are not compatible with high-quality trail experiences.

11. Plan and Act Locally -- Whenever possible, address issues regarding multiple-use trails at the local level (Keller 1990; Kulla 1991). This allows greater sensitivity to local needs and provides better flexibility for addressing difficult issues on a case-by-case basis. Local action also facilitates involvement of the people who will be most affected by the decisions and most able to assist in their successful implementation.

12. Monitor Progress -- Monitor the ongoing effectiveness of the decisions made and programs implemented. It is essential to evaluate the effectiveness of the actions designed to minimize conflicts; provide for safe, high-quality trail experiences; and protect natural resources. Conscious, deliberate monitoring is the only way to determine if conflicts are indeed being reduced and what changes in programs might be needed. This is only possible within the context of clearly understood and agreed-upon objectives for each trail area. Two existing visitor impact management frameworks do consider area objectives and offer great potential for monitoring trail settings and trail use impacts:

* Visitor Impact Management System (VIM) -- This model, developed for the National Park Service by the National Park and Conservation Association, assists managers in setting objectives, selecting impact indicators, and monitoring impacts against measurable standards set for each area (Graefe, Kuss and Vaske 1990).

* Limits of Acceptable Change (LAC) -- This system was developed by and for the USDA Forest Service and operates much like the VIM framework (Stankey, Cole and Lucas 1985).

II. RESEARCH NEEDS IN AVOIDING AND MINIMIZING CONFLICTS ON MULTIPLE-USE TRAILS

Part I of this document reviewed and synthesized the existing research and state of the practice regarding conflicts on multiple-use trails. This review revealed gaps in our present understanding of how to avoid and resolve conflicts on multiple-use trails. The following section identifies research questions that could be examined in order to fill these gaps in what we know. Some of the suggested research is theoretical in nature, and some is suggested for applied experimentation by managers in the field. Part II is organized around an outline similar to that used for Part I:

A. The Challenges Faced by Multiple-Use Trail Managers

Maintaining User Safety

Protecting Natural Resources

Providing High-Quality User Experiences

B. Ways to Avoid or Minimize Conflicts on Multiple-Use Trails

Physical Responses

Management Responses

Information and Education

User Involvement

Regulations and Enforcement

Overall Approach

Other Research Needs

There is some overlap among the research topics suggested in these sections, and no attempt has been made to put the suggestions in any priority order.

A. The Challenges Faced by Multiple-Use Trail Managers

Maintaining User Safety

Develop a more uniform and acceptable "passing alert" word or phrase for faster users to use to alert others (regardless of their activity) of their desire to pass. "Passing on the left," "Excuse me," "Thank you," and many others are possibilities (Kulla 1991).

How to pass other users (from ahead and behind) in the least intrusive ways possible should be examined. How to alert other users and when to do so should be examined from the perspective of the person being passed. This applies to passing other types of users or passing people engaged in the same activity.

What are the stopping distances and safe operating speeds of various trail travel modes under various trail conditions? These data could be used to better establish or justify safe operating speeds and \line speed limits.

It has been suggested that bells be supplied on new bikes as standard equipment (Kulla 1991). How accepted are bells by trail bicyclists? Are bells effective safety equipment when used? How should bikers be instructed to use bells to alert others of their intention to pass? Would a new, more stylish bell design (or other sound-making device) encourage more riders to install and use them? Would some other sound-making device be more effective or accepted?

Protecting Natural Resources

Better studies of the environmental impacts (on soils, wildlife, vegetation, water quality, air quality, etc.) of various trail activities in different environments and under different conditions are needed. Although some fear that such research would fuel unconstructive arguments about "who causes the most damage," a better understanding of what and how damage occurs under different conditions could help in designing and targeting physical and management strategies to minimize impacts.

A "Statement of Principles Concerning Multi-Use Recreational Trails by Non-Motorized Users" (as presented in Keller 1990, 39) calls on Federal and State land management agencies to "undertake a cooperative research project to comprehensively analyze the impact of different users on different types of trails and other users, together with the development of a handbook on trail design practices that can help accommodate multiple user types" (Keller 1990).

Guidelines and procedures for assessing environmental impact and public safety in an objective way are called for by Keller (1990). The Visitor Impact Management (VIM)

(Graefe, Kuss, and Vaske 1990) and Limits of Acceptable Change (LAC) (Stankey, Cole, and Lucas 1985) approaches would be excellent frameworks to apply to trail environments. Test applications of these approaches should be undertaken for trail systems of different types in different parts of the country.

More research and experimentation on the merits of dispersed versus concentrated use should be undertaken (Cole 1986). Experiments comparing these two strategies for trails are needed to better understand the relationship between trail use levels and impacts.

Providing High-Quality User Experiences

More theoretical research is needed to understand and define what conflict is. The best definitions should be refined and applied specifically to trail-based recreation so that managers, users, and researchers can improve understanding and communication in this area.

Better ways to actually measure and evaluate conflicts, as well as satisfaction, are needed. Meaningful comparisons across studies will not be possible until more valid and reliable instruments are available. Measurement tools more in line with the definition proposed by Jacob and Schreyer (1980) would be most helpful (Watson et al. in press).

We need to understand how recreationists go about determining how satisfied they are with a certain experience. In particular, how and to what extent are their feelings and emotions attributable to the product, the individual, and the situation (Williams 1988).

Studies that determine the types of experiences different types of users are seeking would be useful to managers as they attempt to provide opportunities for those experiences. For example, are the users of a particular park more interested in solitude or challenge on the trails?

What are the norms (standards of behavior) of various trail groups? How consistent and stable are these norms among participants in various activities and within various geographic trail areas? How different are these norms among conflicting groups? We cannot effectively attempt to modify behavior or influence norms until we have a better understanding of just what each group considers to be inappropriate behavior in various situations. How are the normative "rules" for trail areas established (Owens 1985)?

Substituting another site or activity is thought to be a common coping strategy employed by trail users who experience conflict. More research, especially leading to improved theory, is needed on recreation substitution.

What factors are *most* important to how sensitive a trail user is to conflict -- individual differences, situational factors, or activity influences?

Do individuals and groups that are experiencing conflict perceive trail areas and the purposes of these areas differently? In what ways?

Existing theoretical models of what causes conflict need to be better tested so that managers can understand and thereby anticipate conflict before it becomes entrenched (Owens 1985).

What is the relationship between satisfaction (and conflict) and the density of other users? Is the behavior of other trail users more important than the number of others on the trail (Owens 1985)?

Research involving long-term monitoring of areas is needed to see if conflict is really distinct from crowding. Owens (1985) suggests that this would be best undertaken in intensively used areas where some users are dependent upon that particular resource.

More research should examine the relative importance of social and psychological aspects of conflict versus the physical aspects (e.g., competition for resources) of conflict.

What psychological processes take place when the normative "rules" of an area are broken (Owens 1985)?

A better understanding of the coping strategies trail users employ is needed. What are these strategies; how and when are they triggered? How can we better predict displacement, substitution, and dissatisfaction caused by conflict so we can manage accordingly?

Coping strategies to reduce conflict are thought to change the recreation experience for those needing to employ them. What are these changes, and how do they occur?

More studies of conflict are needed in nonwilderness and nonbackcountry locations.

Who are the most conflict-sensitive users, and what makes them different from others (Owens 1985)?

What is happening to the most conflict-sensitive users? Are they being displaced, accepting second-rate places and times, or staying and having less satisfying experiences (Owens 1985)?

Studies of the long-term users of an area might be revealing. Are they continuing to use the area because they are the most tolerant and are experiencing little conflict, or are they experiencing high conflict and are just unwilling to substitute other times or places (Owens 1985)?

To what extent is conflict related to personal characteristics, level of commitment, and level of experience (Owens 1985)?

B. Ways to Avoid or Minimize Conflicts on Multiple-Use Trails

Physical Responses

The best and most natural ways to screen trails for sight, sound, smell, etc., should be determined. This could help reduce the level, duration, and intensity of trail-user contacts.

Better research should be conducted regarding the durability of different trail surface materials.

More research into the best ways to control and repair erosion is needed along with a better understanding of how to protect and restore vegetation. Important criteria for all these techniques are that they be natural-looking, safe, and as unobtrusive as possible.

How are speeds and use patterns affected by different trail widths, surfaces, shoulders, signs, etc.? For example, what are the best widths for greenways in various environments and at various expected use levels?

A thorough review of American Association of State Highway and Transportation Officials (AASHTO) standards should be conducted to determine if they can be improved to avoid and reduce trail-user conflicts more effectively.

Better empirical data on the behavior of trail users is needed to improve design and safety standards. Some of these could be modeled after studies conducted by the auto industry.

Continued advances in reducing noise and pollution levels of motorized trail vehicles are needed.

Management Responses

Information and Education -- What are the best and most cost-effective means of communicating with trail users? What are the most effective means of unobtrusively influencing the attitudes and behaviors of trail users? Research should be conducted on which modes (e.g., brochures, signs, volunteer trail patrols, uniformed officers, etc.) and what messages (e.g., positive, negative, short, long, etc.) are most effective in influencing attitudes and changing the behavior of trail users.

Better ways to provide information to users early in their trips and during their trip-planning process should be developed. Computerized systems should be considered for this purpose (Roggenbuck and Ham 1986).

We need to improve our understanding of users' characteristics, behavior, and information needs. This will aid in the development of information programs (Roggenbuck and Ham 1986).

Who are the users within each user group who are most in need of behavior changes?

Which users are most likely to be uninformed or commit unintentional, unskilled, or careless acts that lead to conflict?

What are the characteristics of "renegade" users, and how can they best be targeted and reached?

What are the best ways to break down false impressions different user groups often hold of one another? How can we get users to appreciate (or try) activities that are new to them?

Research on the extent of crossover among different trail activities is needed. Watson, Williams, and Daigle (1991) found that mountain bike riders in certain parts of the Rattlesnake National Recreation Area were similar to hikers in many respects. Determining the similarities among different user groups and documenting the extent to which trail users participate in multiple trail activities could ease "us and them" feelings and reduce conflict.

How can manufacturers of trail-related equipment and supplies be encouraged to become more involved in education programs, resolving conflicts, and helping to address other trail issues? Is a bike shop or manufacturer "tax" on new mountain bikes or a license fee feasible and acceptable (Kulla 1991)?

More uniform trail ethics or etiquette guidelines should be developed (Kulla 1991). The perspectives of all major user groups need to be considered when drafting these.

User Involvement -- What are the barriers to users becoming involved in trail clubs and trail coalitions? What are the best ways to involve the public in long-term, constructive trail efforts? How effective are trail outings, on-trail work projects, meetings, working groups, etc., in this regard? What skills do managers need to involve the public effectively in planning and managing trails for \line shared use?

Regulations and Enforcement -- How can trail speed limits most effectively be enforced?

Experiments with personal identification of trail users (suggested by Sharon Saare and related in Keller 1990) should be carried out. Name tags, license plates, or other means could be tried in problem areas to encourage accountability and responsibility. It might also be worth experimenting with messages similar to the "I'm a professional, how's my driving?" stickers on many commercial trucks. Trail groups might produce and market tee shirts, buttons, etc., with an "I'm a Responsible Trail User -- How's my Riding (Walking, Skiing, etc.)?" statement.

Overall Approach

What are the tangible issues that result in conflict among and within trail uses? These facts could help users and managers get beyond stereotypes and identify the issues among and between activities that most commonly result in conflict.

Case studies should be conducted comparing approaches and conditions between areas where conflict has been avoided (or managed well) and areas experiencing severe problems with user conflict. Such research could begin to objectively identify promising approaches and favorable conditions for successful trail sharing.

Conflict resolution and conflict avoidance success stories for multiple-use trails should be better documented and publicized.

Chavez, Winter, and Baas (1993) suggest a national exchange of ideas among land managers to help establish what works regarding mountain bike management in various areas and under various conditions.

How effective would various professional conflict resolution and binding arbitration techniques be in cases of intense conflicts between user groups in particular areas?

Other Research Needs

More accurate and cost-effective ways to measure trail use levels are needed (Krumpe and Lucas 1986). Similarly, more accurate and cost-effective ways to gather trail use and trail impact information need to be developed. These methods should gather information on manageable user characteristics such as party size, length of stay, activities, time of use, distribution of use, etc. (Kuss et al. 1990).

What are the long-term participation patterns of trail users in terms of frequency, types of trips, and activities? How common is it for users to change activities over time?

What are the trends in terms of trail activities and patterns of use? What will be the most popular activities at various points in the future? What new activities are emerging that managers will need to plan for?

What are the best ways to anticipate how popular particular emerging trail activities will become? What are the best ways to predict the levels and types of use particular trails will receive?

C. Conclusion

The research suggested above covers a very wide range of topics. Some of these topics will interest university-based researchers while others will be more intriguing to trail managers working in the field. Some will be priorities for both. Identifying the most pressing studies and forging the partnerships necessary to carry them out will require communication, cooperation, and time. It will also require resources in terms of staff, money, and equipment. Improving our ability to avoid and manage conflicts on trails will not be easy, and it will not be quick. However, improved trail safety, natural resource protection, and trail experiences for users will make it worth the effort.

Appendix 1

National Recreational Trails Advisory Committee

Government (Chair)
Stuart H. Macdonald
State Trails Coordinator
Division of Parks & Outdoor Recreation
1313 Sherman Street, Rm 618
Denver, CO 80203
(303) 866-3203 ext 306
FAX (303) 866-3206

4-Wheel Driving
Henry Agonia
North Bakersfield Recreation and Park District
405 Galaxy Avenue
Bakersfield, CA 93308
(805) 392 2000
FAX (805) 392-2041

Disabilities
Jeffrey L. Butson
State of Wisconsin, State Trails Council
5002 Sheboygon Avenue #148
Madison, WI 53705
(608) 266-9600
FAX (608) 266-3957

Snowmobiling
Donald M. Carlson
2649 Randy Avenue
White Bear Lake, MN 55110
(612) 429-1041

Bicycling
Bill Flournoy
Chief, Environmental Assessment
North Carolina Dept. of Environment, Health and Natural Resources
P.O. Box 27687
Raleigh, NC 27611
(919) 715 4191
FAX (919) 733-2622

Water Trail
Bruce T. Kerfoot

750 Gunflint Trail
Grand Marais, MN 55604
(218) 388-2294
FAX (218) 388-9429

All-Terrain Vehicle Riding
George M. Lear
15119 Old Dale Road
Centreville, VA 22020
(703) 818-7169

Equestrian
Roberta "Bobbi" Lipka
American Horse Council Director
6171 Chili Riga Center Rd.
Churchville, NY 14428
(716) 293 2561

Cross-Country Skiing
Anne Lusk
Vermont Trails & Greenways Council
1531 River Road
Stowe, VT 05672
(802) 253 7758
FAX (802) 244-1481

Hunting & Fishing
Loren Lutz
3113 Mesaloa Lane
Pasadena, CA 91107
(818) 797 1287

Hiking
Bernice E. Paige
Idaho Trails Council
P.O. Box 1629
Sun Valley, ID 83353
(208) 622-3046

Off-Road Motorcycling
Roger C. Pattison
Clovis Sportcycle Association, Inc.
P.O. Box 2007

Clovis, NM 88101
(505) 389-5269
FAX (505) 389-5357

Appendix 2

Organizations to Contact for Additional Information

Adventure Cycling Association
(formerly Bikecentennial)
P.O. Box 8308
Missoula, MT 59807
(406) 721-1776

American Hiking Society
P.O. Box 20160
Washington, DC 20041
(703) 255-9304

American Honda
1919 Torrance Boulevard
Torrance, CA 90501-2746
(310) 783-3786

American Horse Council
1700 K Street, NW
Washington, DC 20006
(202) 296-4031

Appalachian Mountain Club
5 Joy Street
Boston, MA 02108
(617) 523-0636

Appalachian Trail Conference
P.O. Box 236
Harpers Ferry, WV 25425
(304) 535-6331

Arizona State Parks
1300 W. Washington
Phoenix, AZ 85007
(602) 542-4174

Back Country Horsemen of America
P.O. Box 597
Columbia Falls, MT 59912
(406) 755-2014

Backcountry Horsemen of Idaho

P.O. Box 513
Salmon, ID 83467

Backcountry Horsemen of Washington
P.O. Box 563
Leavenworth, WA 98826
(509) 763-3470

Backcountry Horsemen of Washington
Olympic Chapter
P.O. Box 434
Burley, WA 98322

Bay Area Ridge Trail Council
311 California Street, Suite 300
San Francisco, CA 94104
(415) 391-0697

Bicycle Federation of America (BFA)
1506 21st Street, NW, Suite 200
Washington, DC 20036
(202) 463-6622

Bicycling Magazine
C/O Rodale Press
P.O. Box 6098
Emmaus, PA 18098
(800) 845-8050

Blue Ribbon Coalition
P.O. Box 5449
Pocatello, ID 83202
(208) 237-1557

California Department of Parks and
Recreation
Off-Highway Motor Vehicle Recreation Division
P.O. Box 942896
Sacramento, CA 94296-0001
(916) 653-9072

Cascade Bike Club
(206) 522-3222
For recording, 206-522-BIKE

East Bay Regional Park District

2950 Peralta Oaks Court
P.O. Box 5381
Oakland, CA 94605-0381
(510) 635-0135

Greenways, Inc.
121 Edinburgh South, Suite 210
Cary, NC 27511
(919) 380-0127

Idaho Department of Parks and Recreation
Statehouse Mail
Boise, ID 83720-8000

Idaho Trails Council
P.O. Box 1629
Sun Valley, ID 83353
(208) 622-3046

International Mountain Bicycling Association (IMBA)
P.O. Box 7578
Boulder, CO 80306-7578
(303) 545-9011

International Snowmobile Council
3975 University Drive, Suite 310
Fairfax, VA 22030
(703) 273-9606

International Snowmobile Industry
Association
3975 University Drive, Suite 310
Fairfax, VA 22030
(703) 273-9606

Izaac Walton League of America
1401 Wilson Blvd., Level B
Arlington, VA 22209
(703) 528-1818

Izaac Walton League of America
Milwaukee Chapter
3540 N. Maryland Avenue
Shorewood, WI 53211

League of American Bicyclists
(formerly League of American Wheelmen)
190 W. Ostend St., Suite 120
Baltimore, MD 21230
(410) 539-3399

Low Impact Mountain Bicyclists of Missoula (LIMB)
P.O. Box 2896
Missoula, MT 59806

Metro Trail System Committee
6631 South University Blvd.
Littleton, CO 80121
(303) 795-6531

Midpeninsula Regional Open Space District
330 Distel Circle
Los Altos, CA 94022-1404
(415) 691-1200

Motorcycle Industry Council, Inc.
2 Jenner Street, Suite 150
Irvine, CA 92718
(714) 727-4211

National Off-Highway Vehicle Conservation Council
P.O. Box 2225
Torrance, CA 90509-2225
(310) 783-3888

National Off-Road Bicycling Association (NORBA)
1 Olympic Plaza
Colorado Springs, CO 80909
(719) 578-4717

National Park Service\emdash Rivers, Trails, and Conservation Assistance Program
800 North Capitol St. NW, Suite 490
Washington, DC 20001
(202) 343-3780

National Outdoor Leadership School (NOLS)
288 Main Street

Lander, WY
(307) 332-6973

National Snowmobile Foundation
3975 University Drive, Suite 310
Fairfax, Virginia 22030
(703) 273-9606

New England Mountain Bike Association (NEMBA)
69 Spring Street
Cambridge, MA 02141

Pima County Parks and Recreation
1204 West Silverlake
Tucson, AZ 85713
(602) 740-2690

PIMA Trails Association
5660 Paseo de la Tirada
Tucson, AZ 85715
(602) 577-2095

Rails-to-Trails Conservancy
1400 16th Street NW, Suite 300
Washington, DC 20036
(202) 797-5400

Recreational Equipment, Inc.
P.O. Box 88125
Seattle, WA 98138-2125
(800) 426-4840

Responsible Snowmobiling Program
(Steer Clear Campaign)
735 North Water Street, Suite 618
Milwaukee, Wisconsin 53202
(414) 276-4242

Southern Arizona Mountain Bike Association (SAMBA)
3232 East Speedway
Tucson, AZ 85715
(602) 327-3232

Specialty Vehicle Institute of America
2 Jenner Street, Suite 150
Irving, CA 92718

(714) 727-3727

Steer Clear\emdash Responsible
Snowmobiling Program
625 North Milwaukee Street
Milwaukee, Wisconsin 53202
(414) 276-4242

Tread Lightly! Inc.
Suite 325-C
298-24th Street
Ogden, Utah 84401
1-800-966-9900
(801) 627-0077

United Four Wheel Drive Associations, Inc.
4505 W. 700 So.
Shelbyville, IN 46176

United States Ski Association
Box 777
Brattleboro, VT 05301

Urban Edges
1401 Blake Street, Suite 301
Denver, CO 80202
(303) 623-8107

U.S. Department of Agriculture
Forest Service
America\rquote s Great Outdoors, Suite 726
1331 Pennsylvania Ave., NW
Washington, DC 20090

U.S. Department of Agriculture
Forest Service
Northern Region
P.O. Box 7669
Missoula, MT 59807
(406) 329-3711

U.S. Department of Interior
Bureau of Land Management
Unlimited Outdoor Adventure
Washington, DC 20240

Utah Department of Natural Resources
1636 West North Temple
Salt Lake City, UT 84111

Utah Mountain Bike Association (UMBA)
476 East South Temple, Suite 246
Salt Lake City, UT 84111
(801) 531-7703

Appendix 3

Persons Contributing Information for This Report

Steve Anderson
PIMA Trails Association
(602) 296-2260

Harry Baker
CA 4WD Clubs Inc.
(818) 705-3930

Attila Bality
National Park Service
(505) 988-6775

Mike Barrow
Boulder Off-Road Alliance
(303) 924-2730

Ron Blakemore
Ventura County, CA
(805) 654-3962

Peter Bluhon
Bay Area Ridge Trail
(510) 236-7435

Brent Botts
USDA Forest Service
(202) 205-1313

Jude Carino
Bureau of Land Management
(307) 261-7600

Debbie Chavez
Pacific SW Experiment Station\emdash USDA
(909) 276-6285

Clark Collins
Blue Ribbon Coalition
(208) 237-1557

Dan Collins

Trails & Waterways Unit
DNR St. Paul MN
(612) 296-6048

Adena Cook
Blue Ribbon Coalition
(208) 522-7339

Jeff Cook
Idaho Parks and Recreation
(208) 327-7444

Jim Cooper
Bureau of Land Management
(707) 462-3873

Tom Crimmins
USDA Forest Service Region 5 OHV
(415) 275-2361

Cynthia D'Agosta
Los Angeles Parks and Recreation
(213) 738-2973

Rob Dingman
Motorcycle Industry Council
(703) 416-0444

Robert Doyle
East Bay Regional Park District
(510) 635-0135

Steve Elkinton
National Park Service
(202) 343-3776

George Ely
Rails-To-Trails Conservancy of Pennsylvania
(717) 774-2929

John Escobar
MidPeninsula Open Space District
(415) 691-0485

Steve Fiala

East Bay Regional Park District
(510) 635-0135

Mylon Filkins
Backcountry Horsemen of America
(805)-832-1150

Chuck Flink
Greenways, Inc.
(919) 380-0127

Chris Frado
Cross Country Ski Areas Association
(603) 239-4341

Barrie Freeman
(ROMP and STOMP event organizer)
(415) 949-3137

Pam Gilmore
Arizona State Parks
(602) 542-1996

Alan Goldman
Bike Council of Marin
(415) 543-3749

Alan Graefe
Pennsylvania State University
(814) 863-8986

Nora Hamilton
USDA Forest Service
(707) 275-2361

David Hammer
Wisconsin State Parks, DNR
(608) 264-6034

Bob Hammond
N. Virginia Trail Riders
(202) 258-1098

Randy Harden
National Off-Highway Vehicle

Conservation Council
(414) 458-3000

Bill Harris
CO Plateau Mountain Biking Trail Association
(303) 249-8055

Jim Hasenauer
International Mountain Bike Association (IMBA)
(818) 704-7396

Susan Henley
American Hiking Association
(703) 255-9304

Susan Henry
Oklahoma Tourism & Recreation Dept.
(405) 521-2973

Charles Huppuch
USDA Forest Service
(404) 347-7392

Scott Iverson
East Bay Regional Park District
(510) 635-0135

Mark Ivy
Delaware Div. of Parks & Recreation
(302) 739-5285

Michael Kelley
International Mountain Bicycling Association (IMBA)
(510) 528-2453

Bill Kruszka
George Washington National Forest
(703) 904-4101

Alan Lane
Indiana 4WD Association
(812) 477-7871

Ursula Lemanski
National Park Service
(202) 343-3766

Bob Lilly
San Juan National Forest
(303) 385-1201

Amy Mann
American Horse Council
(202) 296-4031

Bill Manning
Trails 2000
(303) 259-4682

Mike McCoy
Adventure Cycling Association
(formerly Bikecentennial)
(406) 721-1776

Pennie McEdward-Rand
Catamount Trails Association
(802) 864-5794

Roy Muth
Coalition for Recreation Trails
(703) 273-9606

Katherine Nichols
Texas Parks & Wildlife
(512) 389-4680

Elizabeth Owen
Bureau of Land Management
(202) 452-7796

Hank Park
Rails-To-Trails Conservancy
(202) 797-5400

Wayne Pelkey
VT Association of Snow Travelers
(802) 229-4202

Paul Peterson

Professional Ski Instructors
(209) 753-2834

Elizabeth Porter
National Park Service
(202) 343-3766

Bob Proudman
Appalachian Trail Conference
(304) 535-6331

Reuben Rajala
Trailworks
(603) 466-3668

Barbara Rice
Bay Area Ridge Trail
(415) 391-0697

Karen-Lee Ryan
Rails-To-Trails Conservancy
(202) 797-5400

Jim Schmid
Coronodo National Forest
(602) 670-4513

John Schmill
Dept. of Parks and Recreation, CA
(916) 653-4976

Jeanne Scholl
Boulder Mountain Parks
(303) 441-3408

Robert Searns
Urban Edges
(303) 623-8107

Barbara Sharrow
Bureau of Land Management
(303) 239-3733

Michael Schuett

South West Texas State University
(512) 245-3480

Mike Singleton
KTU & A Consulting
(619) 452-2828

Paul Slavik
American Honda
(310) 783-3786

Dean Swickart
Bureau of Land Management
Folsom Resource Area, CA

Merle Van Horne
National Park Service
(202) 343-3780

Bob Walker
Montana Fish & Wildlife
(406) 444-4585

Bruce Ward
American Hiking Society
(703) 255-9304

Bob Wetzel
Stanislaus National Forest
(209) 795-1381

Lauren Whitehead
Saguaro National Monument
(602) 670-6680

Charlie Willard
California Department of Parks and Recreation
(916) 653-8803

Jim Williams
Motorcycle Industry Council
(714) 727-4211

Curtis Yates
North Carolina State Bicycle Program

(919) 733-2804

Appendix 4

List of Existing Trail-Sharing Guidelines and Other Educational Materials

The following are examples of trail-sharing guidelines and other educational materials designed to help reduce conflict on trails. The type of material and the organization from which it can be obtained are listed after the title of each. The addresses a nd phone numbers of these organizations are included in Appendix 2.

"A Snowmobiler's Code of Ethics"
Ten snowmobile use guidelines available from International Snowmobile Industry Association.

"Back Country Horsemen Commandments"
Seven guidelines available from Backcountry Horsemen of Washington, Olympic Chapter.

" Backcountry Trail Etiquette -- Minimum Impact and Common Courtesy"
Brochure available from Idaho Trails Council.

" Be a Credit to Our Sport"
Ten mountain biking guidelines contained in Mountain Bike Destinations Guide 1990 (1989, by the editors of Mountain Bike Magazine, Rodale Press, Inc., Emmaus, PA 18098).

" Crested Butte's High Country -- To Share and Enjoy"
Brochure available from USDA Forest Service and local ranchers.

" Horse Sense on National Forest Pack Trips"
Brochure available from USDA Forest Service, Northern Region.

" In Their Shoes"
Video and accompanying written scenarios for role-playing and small group discussion. Available for a fee from Arizona State Committee on Trails (ASCOT) through Arizona State Parks.

" Keeping the 'Wild' in Wilderness"
Brochure available from USDA Forest Service, Northern Region.

" Know the Right Way to Bicycle Off-Road"
Two-sided " rack-card"available from the Utah Mountain Bike Association (UMBA) and the Utah Department of Natural Resources.

" Leave No Trace Land Ethics"
Brochure available from the National Outdoor Leadership School (NOLS).

" Low Impact Mountain Bicycling Education Packet"
Video and other materials available for a fee from Low Impact Mountain Bicyclists (LIMB) of Missoula .

" Mountain Bicycling Etiquette"
Flier available from Low Impact Mountain Bicyclists (LIMB) of Missoula, USDA Forest Service, and Adventure Cycling Association (formerly Bikecentennial).

" Mountain Bike FYI"
Brochure available from Recreational Equipment, Inc. (REI).

" Mountain Manners -- A Stock User's Guide to Common Sense and Courtesy in the Back Country"
Brochure available from Backcountry Horsemen of Idaho, Nez Perce National Forest, Idaho Horse Board, Idaho Outfitters and Guides Association.

" Multiple Use Trail Guidelines"
Sign presenting the " IMBA Triangle"of which users should yield to whom.Available from International Mountain Bicycling Association (IMBA).

" Off-Road Cyclist's Code"
Ten guidelines available in various forms from National Off-Road Bicycle Association (NORBA).

" Operation RPM: Riders Pledge Moderation"
Educational program and snowmobile etiquette guidelines available from International Snowmobile Council.

" Pathways Are for Everyone"
Two-sided " rack-card"available from Idaho Department of Parks and Recreation and Idaho Trails Council.

" Recreation Code of Ethics"
Eleven recreational use guidelines available in several forms from Blue Ribbon Coalition.

" Responsible Trail Use Rules"
Card available from East Bay Regional Park District, Metropolitan Horsemen's Association, and Bicycle Trails Council.

" RightRider -- Trail Etiquette"
Brochure (No. 1 in a series) available from Motorcycle Industry Council, USDA Forest Service, Bureau of Land Management, American Horse Council, and Specialty Vehicle Institute of America.

" Rules of the Trail"
Six trail use guidelines available in many forms from International Mountain Bicycling Association (IMBA).

" Rules Off the Road"
Brochure available from Bicycling Magazine.

" Share the Trail -- Enjoying Your Mountain Bike, Preserving the Land"
Brochure available from International Mountain Bicycling Association (IMBA) and Specialized Bicycle Components, Inc.

" Share the Trail!"
Brochure available from The Izaak Walton League of America, Wisconsin Chapter.

" Share the Trails"
Brochure available from New England Mountain Bike Association (NEMBA).

" Sharing the River Park Trail System"
Brochure available from Pima County Parks and Recreation Department, AZ.

" Sharing the Trail! -- A Brochure on Wise Trail Use"
Brochure available from Arizona State Parks, Arizona Hiking and Equestrian Trails Committee, USDA Forest Service, and Recreational Equipment, Inc.

" Sharing the Trails -- Guidelines for: Bicyclists, Dog Owners, Equestrians, Hikers and Runners"
Brochure available from Midpeninsula Regional Open Space District, Los Altos, CA.

" Steer Clear -- Responsible Snowmobiling Program"
Brochure available from Responsible Snowmobiling Program, Milwaukee, Wisconsin.

" The Rules of the Trail"
Flier available from PIMA Trails Association and Southern Arizona Mountain Bike Association (SAMBA).

" Trail Mix"
Brochure available from California Department of Parks and Recreation, Off-Highway Motor Vehicle Recreation Division.

" Trail Safety"
Brochure available from East Bay Regional Park District, CA.

" Trail Safety and Ethics Guidelines"
Contained in Arizona State Trails Guide available from Arizona Hiking and Equestrian

Trails Committee, Arizona State Parks.

" Trails Are for Everyone"
Brochure available from Metro Trail System Committee, Denver.

" Tread Lightly Crew"
Brochure available from Backcountry Horsemen of Washington.

" TREAD LIGHTLY on Public and Private Lands -- A Land Use Ethics Program"
Booklet available from TREAD LIGHTLY! Inc.

" Winter Recreation Code of Ethics"
Ten guidelines available from the International Snowmobile Council.